Animal Byproducts Utilization through Semi-Moist Rendering

By
Mahendra Kumar

2007
DAYA PUBLISHING HOUSE
Delhi - 110 035

ISBN 81-7035-514-1

Published by : **Daya Publishing House**
1123/74, Deva Ram Park
Tri Nagar, Delhi - 110 035
Phone: 27383999
Fax: (011) 23244987
e-mail : dayabooks@vsnl.com
website : www.dayabooks.com

Showroom : 4760-61/23, Ansari Road, Darya Ganj,
New Delhi - 110 002
Phone: 23245578, 23244987

Laser Typesetting : **Classic Computer Services**
Delhi - 110 035

Printed at : **Chawla Offset Printers**
Delhi - 110 052

PRINTED IN INDIA

Dedication

This book is dedicated to my wife, Kusum Agarwal, without whose patience and cooperation this work would not have been possible. From it's conceptualization in 1970 till the field trials of the concept for a brief period in 1988 and thereafter completion and perfection of the technology from 1991 to 1994 at the field station at Bakshi-Ka-Talab, she had to face long periods of separation and isolation at Madras. However, her strength laid in her belief that if the little bit of work being carried out is going to be of any use to the people, it will be a rich reward to her. I wish her expectations are fulfilled through this piece of work.

Mahendra Kumar

Acknowledgements

First and foremost, my thoughts go to those innumerable people who kindled the importance of fallen carcass recovery in my mind. As a student of Leather Technology of University of Madras from 1956 to 1958 and later staff of Central Leather Research Institute (CLRI) from 1963 onwards until my retirement in 1994, I had the opportunity to attend seminars called "Tanners-get-together" extending upto 4 to 5 days organized by CLRI annually. Representatives of industry, research institutes and organizations connected with leather both from India and abroad participated in this event. Irrespective of the subject of the seminar of the year, waste of carcass due to lack of technology would somehow surreptitiously crop in for discussions invariably raised by representatives of Khadi Commission and Khadi Boards. This not only convinced me of the importance but also strengthened my resolve to find a solution to the problem. I feel greatly indebted to all those who ignited this desire in me.

Way back in June, 1969 I arrived Australia for a period of 9 months on a Colombo Plan Fellowship in the area of Animal Wastes utilization. During this period, I visited / worked in about 52 establishments making use of different kinds of animal wastes. This exposure provided an opportunity to thoroughly learn of the basic principles involved in the art of rendering which obviously had been handy in developing the new Semi-Moist Rendering. I express my sincere thanks to the Commonwealth Government of Australia for providing the Fellowship.

A very crucial role was later played by the Food and Agriculture Organization (FAO) of the United Nations. Under the aegis of the Organization, I had been fortunate to work as consultant in the area of hides and skins and animal wastes utilization to Governments of a number of African and Asian countries and also visits to facilities of animal byproducts utilization of many developed countries. The consultancies provided an opportunity to learn that almost all the animal byproducts available in Asian and African developing countries are being wasted or not optimally utilized and visits gave an insight that the rendering technologies in vogue in the developed world are not suitable for the needs of developing countries in general. In fact, equipped with this background, the seed for the design of semi-moist rendering vessel had already been sown in Zaria in Northern Nigeria through a sterilization vessel which I designed and got fabricated locally while working on an FAO consultancy. Let me express my gratefulness to FAO for exposing me to realities.

My work place, CLRI, has been an unique experience. It is not only where the idea developed and germinated but it also provided an environment where one has full liberty to work upon any worthwhile idea. And along with it, the management and a band of dedicated colleagues who are always willing to understand you and be helpful. My salutations to this great institution.

Dr. S. K. Barat needs separate mention. After my joining By-products area at CLRI in 1963, I worked under his direct supervision for about 8 years. He was not only an excellent guide but was always ready to help even in your personal problems. His devotion to duty, resoluteness, fairness, fearlessness etc. were examplary, which also helped to shape my own approach in life. This has kept me in good stead all through. I have no proper words to express my gratitude to this great man.

The Department of Biotechnology (DBT), Government of India, provided funds for part R&D work and establishment of field center at Bakshi-ka-Talab (BKT). Without this timely help, it would have been too difficult to organize field center with the Institutes own resources. My sincere thanks to DBT for its crucial monetary inputs.

The State Government of Uttar Pradesh made available infrastructural facilities through its Department of Animal Husbandry at Model Training-cum-production Center (MTPC) at BKT for establishment of the field center. MTPC is an integrated facility where fallen carcasses are already processed following conventional dry rendering. A part of the existing wing of carcass recovery section was modified for the new semi-moist rendering facility. Availability of infrastructural facilities at BKT saved considerable time, money and organizational efforts in the implementation of semi-moist rendering project. Many thanks to the State Government, Department of Animal Husbandry and State Government's staff at BKT- Mr. D.K. Goel and Mr. S.C. Nigam in particular.

Dr. M.C. Upreti, Scientist incharge of the CSIR Polytechnology Centre at Lucknow helped in liasioning on behalf of CLRI with the State Government in establishing semi-moist technology facility at BKT and also provided day to day help in running the center. It is a pleasure for me to acknowledge Dr. Upreti's inputs in a number of ways.

I personally presented the new development to Dr. Don A. Franco, Director of Scientific Services, National Renderers Association in Alexandria (USA) in August 1996. He was not only happy with the presentation but also expressed that the development has filled up a vacuum for processing small quantities of raw materials. He also felt that it should be possible to incorporate the new concept for larger throughputs. I express my grateful thanks to Dr. Don for his continued interest and suggestions with a view to bring the technology to its logical conclusion to benefit mankind.

My suggestion to publish the new development in the form of a book to Prof. Arun Kulshreshtha, Director, NAM S&T Centre in New Delhi found his ready acceptance. He provided all support, suggestions and facilities of the Centre for the preparation of the book. My sincere and heartful thanks to Dr. Kulshreshtha.

Mr. Anil Mittal of Daya Publishing House, New Delhi is publishing this presentation. I take pleasure and highly appreciate Mr. Mittal's cooperation in this venture.

I have a conviction that the new development will influence the Rendering Industry in many ways and that this book will go a long way in achieving that objective.

Mahendra Kumar
E-mail: mahendra_kumar@yahoo.com

Preface

The author of this book, Mahendra Kumar, is without doubt a true visionary, possessing a broad understanding and knowledge of all facets and benefits of the full utilization of animal by-products and processing/rendering technology. His educational background, his professional expertise, and his dedicated passion for the subject are evident through all the chapters of the text. He harvests this knowledge by continuing to explore endlessly innovative technologies that he describes in this comprehensive presentation. Although the technology developed and described is designed to assist the developing countries, the applicability has no limits and could be readily used in all sectors of the world. In essence, industrialized societies with well established rendering system could benefit equally from the technology. A full chapter is devoted in the write up suggesting possible methodology for scaling-up the technology.

The author whom I have had the pleasure to exchange information on emerging technology over the years is a devoted problem-solver, intent on assisting emerging economies on the available options that can be pursued to maximize the full and complete use of animal "waste" into the manufacture of protein feed ingredients and fat as excellent sources of feed supplementation, and the enhancement of agricultural efficiencies. His frustration that the developing countries of Africa, Asia, and other sectors of the world have not taken the initiative to "mimic" some of the successes enjoyed by developed countries is a compelling reason for the publication of this informative book. In essence, this book can be considered a gift by someone who has devoted years to a subject he truly loves and is willing to share so that others could benefit.

From hides and skins to animal "waste" and dedicated service to global organizations like the United Nations, including extensive work within his own country, India, makes Mahendra Kumar, more than qualified to disseminate his knowledge with us in this insightful book, Animal Byproducts utilization through Semi-Moist Rendering.

The topics of the book, consisting of 17 chapters, is full of diversity, covering every conceivable aspect/concept of rendering technology, that if embraced by developing countries could serve as definite assets to enhance the agricultural economy through the acceptance of new options for processing animal "waste". Information throughout the book adds to the limited literature available in rendering technology and would benefit the agricultural sector in developing countries by contributing to the existing void in knowledge of rendering technology and options that are overlooked.

Mahendra Kumar's efforts would be appreciated by all with an interest in agricultural innovations to maximize and optimize the use of material that is currently not fully utilized, especially what is usually deemed animal waste. The book is a must read and will definitely benefit those who are forward-looking and seeking ways to embrace simple technology as a voyage to success. It is especially applicable to developing countries, just as the author intended.

Don A. Franco, DVM, MPH, DACVPM
President,
Centre for Bio-Security, Food Safety and Public Health,
Lake Worth, Florida

Contents

List of Figures

List of Tables

Abbreviations

1. FAO: Food and Agriculture Organisation
2. DBT: Department of Biotechnology
3. MTPC: Model Training-cum-Production Centre
4. RC: Rumen Content
5. RCC: Reinforced Concrete and Cement
6. CLRI: Central Leather Research Institute
7. BSE: Bovine Spongiform Encephalopathy
8. CRC: Carcass Recovery Centre
9. BKT: Bakshi Ka Talab
10. a_w: Water Activity
11. mm: millimeter
12. cm: centimeter
13. m: meter

14. km: Kilometer
15. kg: kilogram
16. °C: Degree Celsius
17. °F: Degree Fahrenheit
18. psi: Pounds per Square Inch
19. p.a.: per annum
20. CNG: Compressed Natural Gas
21. CSIR: Council of Scientific and Industrial Research
22. LPG: Liquified Petroleum Gas

Chapter 1
Introduction

Rendering is a process of subjecting animal offal/tissues to the treatment of heat with a view to melt and extract fat; thereafter, the solids are processed into meat meal, bone meal etc. The rendering processes in vogue can be classified into two categories viz; dry rendering and wet rendering. A new process to be called " Semi-moist Rendering " has been developed by this author and discussed here in detail.

In almost all the developing countries, there is a common problem of either non-utilization or under-utilization of animals dying of natural death (fallen animals) and soft tissues obtainable from slaughterhouses, poultry dressing units and fisheries etc. Because of lack of proper veterinary services and other factors like insufficient supply of feed and fodder, the number of animals dying due to natural death is generally high in almost all the developing countries and hence this constitutes a single largest source of animal based raw material to be processed in any of the countries. For example, according to estimates made during 1986 and 1987, an estimated of 41 million animals (around 25 million bovine and 16 million ovine) die of natural death in India annually and the country suffers a loss of Rs. 6000 million (around US$ 200 million) every year because of under or non- utilization of this resource (Mahendra Kumar 1986 and Report of All India Survey on Hides and Skins 1987). While working at the Central Leather Research Institute (CLRI), the new technology package of semi-moist rendering has been developed for processing of fallen carcasses, specially suited for Indian conditions. The technology is also applicable to the utilization of animal based tissues of all descriptions. The author is of the view that this technology will be equally suitable for other developing countries for processing both fallen carcasses as well as soft tissues with minor modifications, if necessary, as to be suitable to the conditions of the respective countries. Under specific conditions, the package is likely to find application in some of the developed countries as well.

An attempt has been made to discuss the new technological package developed, which is economically viable as well as simple, low cost, zero waste, environmentally clean and eco-friendly. The present state of the art of carcass utilization in India, some of the serious technological and organizational problems which this sector faces and suggestions to overcome these problems have also been discussed with a belief that very similar problems may be prevailing in other developing countries and the suggestions made to overcome such problems, may work as guidelines to find solutions in the respective countries. Few possible fallouts outs of the technology and their applications in related areas have been offered.

Brief discussion on conventional wet rendering and dry rendering processes has been offered to enable the reader to compare the simplicity as well as cost structure of semi-moist rendering to the conventional technologies.

Theoretical and practical aspects for production of compost and vermicompost respectively and production of biogas from materials like rumen contents and animal based soft offals have been described.

The problem of BSE in the context of new technology and scaling up of the same for large throughputs have also been briefly discussed.

Detailed information on cost of the project with profitability and brief idea of profitability of maintaining a pig farm are given.

A list of appropriate references has been included.

Chapter 2
Semi Moist Rendering

The classification of rendering processes can be done on the basis of moisture content of tissues, soon after they ensue from rendering; consequently, all the processes in vogue will fall into two categories viz; dry rendering and wet rendering. This author has developed a new process of rendering to be called "Semi-moist Rendering" wherein the moisture of the tissues as they ensue after rendering, falls in between the earlier two kinds of processes of dry rendering and wet rendering. New process apart, the author also developed the whole package of technology, which covers all aspects associated with rendering including treatment of effluents and their utilization etc.

With a variation of about minus 5 per cent, the moisture of the rendered tissues under 3 categories of processes is shown in Table 2.1.

Table 2.1: Moisture of Rendered Tissues Under 3 Categories of Processes

Type of Process	*Percentage of Moisture of Tissues as they Ensue soon after Rendering*	*Percentage of Solids*
Wet Rendering	80	20
Semi-moist Rendering	55	45
Dry Rendering	08	92

Translating the data in Table 2.1 on moisture free basis of the solids, the percentage of moisture held by the respective solids in the three respective processes is shown in Table 2.2.

Table 2.2: Moisture of Rendered Tissues Under 3 Categories of Processes on Moisture-free Basis of the Solids

Type of Process	*Quantity of Tissues as they Ensure soon after Rendering*	*Percentage of Solids held by the Rendered Tissues*	*Percentage of Moisture held by the Solids on Moisture Free Basis*
Wet Rendering	100 weight units	20	400.00
Semi moist Rendering	100 weight units	45	122.20
Dry Rendering	100 weight units	92	8.70

Rendered tissues can be stored safely for reasonably long time at a moisture content of less than 10 per cent. As such, no further drying is necessary for storage of dry rendered produce, known as meat meal. However in the case of wet rendered material, 391.3 (400-8.7) per cent moisture will have to be expelled out to obtain 100 weight units of meat meal of the same as to be at par in moisture content with dry rendered one; as opposed to this, only113.5 (122.2-8.7) per cent moisture will be required to be driven out in the case of semi-moist rendered stuff (Woodley, M 2005).

In other words, almost 3.5 times (391.3/113.5 = 3.44) moisture is required to be driven out of the wet rendered material as compared to semi-moist rendered one; this will mean considerable savings on energy, land and infrastructure costs in the case of semi-moist rendering option. This basic difference becomes the basis for the new process to called "**SEMI MOIST RENDERING**". In case of semi-moist rendering, the costs are further slashed down, because the rendered tissues are to be preserved wet as such, by controlling the water activity.

Considering of costs further, it will be relevant to mention that the reduction of moisture of the meat meal in the case of dry rendering, has not been without the tag of cost addition. Steam has been used to drive out moisture from the rendered tissues as to arrive at a moisture content of around 8 per cent.

Hence cost of production in semi-moist rendering process is considerably lower to either dry rendering or wet rendering.

Chapter 3
State of the Art

3.1 Existing Carcass Processing Centers

During 1983-84, there were about 183 carcass recovery centers in India where a total of 86483 carcasses were processed during the year (Mahendra Kumar 1986). This figure has not changed much since then and is just around 0.2 per cent of the total available fallen carcasses of 41 million annually in the country.

3.2 Technologies in Vogue

There are three types of processes, which are in vogue in the country for making use of the fallen carcasses; these being dry rendering, wet rendering and open pan rendering.

Dry rendering is a good process but unfortunately is not economically viable under Indian conditions because of the huge investment on plant, machinery and infrastructure. As a result, there are hardly three dry rendering plants in the country as a whole and even these are not working satisfactorily. Though the investment on wet rendering equipment is comparatively less (than dry rendering), the process is still not economically viable under Indian conditions. The investment on open pan rendering is low but the end products obtained are of poor quality. However, this is the process of choice in most of the carcass recovery centers in India because of low investment. Detailed information on all the three rendering processes mentioned here is available (Mahendra Kumar 1987).

3.3 Environmental Pollution

Irrespective of which process is followed for carcass recovery in the country, the environment around the place of work remains highly polluted and filthy resulting in obnoxious odors and presence of flies, vultures and dogs etc. This is for the fact that effluents from the flaying yard, soluble proteins emanating from the rendering process and rumen contents are not suitably disposed off or put to utilization. These materials decay over the time and cause serious environmental pollution.

3.4 Uneconomic Processes

Generally speaking, the processing of the carcasses by any of the three processes in vogue as mentioned under 3.2, is uneconomic. This is the reason that there are no carcass recovery centers in the country in the private sector. Almost all the existing centers are run or aided by the Khadi and Village Industries Commission and State Khadi and Industries Boards on social cost.

Chapter 4

Problems

The carcass sector is faced with a number of problems both technological and organizational; a good account of it is available in the literature (Mahendra Kumar 1986). Amongst many, the following two look to be most serious and critical.

4.1 Absence of Appropriate Technology

There had been absence of economically viable and environmentally friendly technolcgy to process fallen carcasses under the prevailing conditions in India–rural India in particular.

In India, the livestock is largely raised by individuals, most often for their own needs; farms are scanty. Hence the livestock is well spread over large areas throughout the length and the breadth of the country. As a result, the availability of the raw material (fallen carcass as well as soft tissues from slaughtered animals) at a particular given place and time is rather limited. In most parts of rural India, one may not be able to get more than 3-4 carcasses (in terms of weight it is about half ton of raw material to be processed) per day within a radius of 10-15 kms. With the present conditions of roads and communication systems as available in the country, collection of carcasses beyond this distance proves uneconomic as well as impractical. Hence, the technology should be economically viable for processing 3-4 carcasses per day and, of course, it has to be environmentally clean and eco-friendly from technological angle; this is the minimum requirement to make carcass utilization a reality.

4.2 Absence of Proper Organization

After the animal is dead, traditionally there had been a practice of fallen carcasses being lifted by the Harijans in almost all parts of the country with a view of its disposal. The carcass was flayed for hide or skin (to be used for leather making) and the rest of the flayed structure left unattended and allowed to be wasted as a way of disposal.

In some of the states, local bodies like Zila Parishads, Municipal Boards and Panchayats have put an end to the traditional practice and in place are selling rights for lifting of the available carcasses in the area of their respective jurisdiction to contractors; this is done by awarding contracts to the highest bidders. Contracts are generally for a period of one year. Institution of contracts is desirable as this ensures supply of raw material on regular basis; normally a minimum of three carcasses and beyond may be available every day in each contracted area. As one is not sure of remaining in business beyond the contract period of one year, he is not prepared to invest on the creation of the necessary infrastructure required for the utilization of the carcasses on proper lines.

The disposal of carcasses should essentially be considered as a social and environmental problem and thereby, all necessary inputs should be made available to this sector to see that the environment is kept clean. Many other things apart, on the organizational side, one of the most important inputs will be to award the contracts on long-term basis (15 years or more) and that too on nominal cost; this will enable the contractors to invest on infrastructure necessary to process the carcass on proper scientific lines. As a matter of fact, it is desirable to award the contracts only to such parties who have either created proper infrastructure or are prepared to do so.

Chapter 5
Some Common Requirements

Irrespective of which technology is to be followed, there are some common requirements, which should always be met with in any carcass utilization program. These are discussed.

5.1 Means of Communication

In the developed economies, the carcass recovery centers are equipped with telephone and walkie-talkie facilities and as such information of the death of the animal could be communicated to the center through these means without loss of time. However, in the developing world, such facilities are not commonly available–rural areas in particular. To overcome this problem, a very practical and innovative system of communication has been evolved in

India. The carcass recovery centers (CRC) have appointed informers in all the villages in the area of their jurisdiction; soon after the death occurs, the concerned informer in the village travels on bicycle to the CRC and informs about the death of the animal. With the advent of Cell Phone and its cheap availability in the country, more people are adopting this fast and affordable technology for communication. After receipt of information, the center organizes the collection and transport of the carcass as fast as possible. Under field conditions as available in India, most of the carcasses usually get collected and transported to the centers within a period of about six hours after the death. As no significant damage occurs to the carcass within 12-15 hours after death, this method of communication has been found quite satisfactory and yet simple and cheap.

5.2 Transport Vehicle

There are certain minimal requirements which a vehicle to be used for collection and transport of the fallen carcasses has to meet; these are as follows:

1. Be suitable for running on rural roads - many times tar roads are not available in rural areas.
2. Lifting, loading and un-loading of the carcasses is done by a single person (driver alone); this will reduce operational cost.
3. Does not have any recurring expenditure while not in use.
4. Cost of the vehicle and running (of the same) is reasonable such that the expenditure on collection is within permissible limits.
5. Should be amenable to repairs in local workshops at reasonable cost.

A locally fabricated four wheel drive, diesel driven vehicle is already in use in rural India; this will meet all the above requirements after it is fitted with a loading and unloading mechanism consisting of pulley and steel rope operated manually with a set of gears. By tugging the carcass to the rope and operation of the gears, the carcass can be loaded on to the vehicle with ease, transported and later unloaded at the CRC (Figure 5.1).

Figure 5.1: Carcass Being Loaded on to the Vehicle

In metropolis of Delhi, Compressed Natural Gas (CNG) run vehicles have proved both cheap on running cost and environmentally clean. Diesel driven four wheel drive vehicles will be replaced by CNG driven vehicles over the time. This will make collection of caracass comparatively cheaper and environmental friendly.

5.3 Water Supply

There has to be abundant supply of potable water. Water is required everywhere—in the flaying yard, watering of plants, toilets, personal hygiene, animal yard and so on. Ideally, it should be stored in an over-head tank so that it is available with some force at the point of delivery; it reduces work and helps in better and faster cleaning of the place or for that matter watering of plants. In addition, storage of some water in a tank raised on the ground has been found very handy in times of failure of power supply. A provision of hand pump will be additional safety.

5.4 Hygiene in Handling

Hygiene is a basic and utmost important requirement, which has to be maintained at all points and in all operations. Yeasts, molds and bacteria are present everywhere in the environment. There has to be an attempt to ideally eliminate or minimize contamination both of the raw material as well as the processed products with microbes from the environment or any other source. To this end, the flaying of the carcass should be done in a manner which is followed under 'dry slaughtering' wherein the dressing of the carcass *viz.*, its flaying, evisceration, splitting and dispatch is done in a way that the flayed carcass does not come in contact with water, hide or viscera etc. (Mann, 1984). Evisceration should, therefore, be done with utmost care so that bowels do not get damaged and contaminate the flayed carcass. Contamination should also be avoided during the operation of chopping of the carcass and loading of the chopped pieces into the rendering vessel; same applies to the separation of bone and soft tissues of the rendered mass, mincing of the soft rendered tissues and mixing of the mince with salt and molasses etc. The tools and equipments used should be properly disinfected after every use and only potable water has to be used.

In many country slaughter houses in the U.K., dry slaughtering is followed. This ensures best possible hygiene during dressing (Goodman, J 1991).

5.5 Clean Environment

There is a great concern these days that the technologies adopted are environmentally clean and eco-friendly. The new technology package as will be discussed in this write up satisfies this requirement.

Environmental pollution had perhaps been one of the major factors, at least in India, for the neglect and non-development of the carcass sector. The surroundings of the existing carcass recovery centers in the country are highly polluted with attendant obnoxious odors, flies, dogs and frequent visits of scavenging birds.

An environmentally clean and eco-friendly technology will give respectability to the profession and thereby help in its adoption by the people.

5.6 Scheduled Diseases

Diseases like anthrax, foot and mouth, rabies, tetanus etc. fall under the category of scheduled diseases in as much as these are communicable to man. Among these, anthrax is the most dreaded one; its spores pose great danger to man, livestock and environment with serious consequences. As such, carcasses of animals dying of anthrax should not be brought to the CRC. These have to be discarded in their entirety and disposed off according to laid down procedures. One of the three methods *viz;* Incineration, Burial or

Anaerobic digestion is recommended for disposal (Mann, I 1984).

Unfortunately, there is no rapid spot test for anthrax. In areas where anthrax is not prevalent, the problem does not exist. However, in regions of incidence (of anthrax), clinical signs like high fever, bloody discharge from natural body openings (like anus and nostrils) and sudden death (cattle in particular) could be the guiding factors. Such carcasses should be discarded and disposed off, even though some of them may not have died of anthrax (Campbell, S.G. 1995). Hence, the personnel responsible for the collection of the fallen stock from the field should find the history of the death of the animal and the carcass disposed off in suspected cases.

As there are various forms of anthrax and different species of animals may show different clinical signs when affected, one is advised to know more about the disease (Otto H. Siegmund *et al.*, 1982).

As a measure of safety and precaution, the personnel working at CRC should be vaccinated against anthrax.

Chapter 6
Unique Features of the Technology

The most striking feature of this package lies in the fact that

1. It is zero waste.
2. Economically viable for small throughputs.
3. Equipments needed can be fabricated locally; thereby no need for imports.
4. Easy maintenance of equipment.
5. Simplest possible in operation.
6. Low investment.
7. Environmentally clean.
8. Eco-friendly.
9. Use of local raw materials.

10. Production of high quality proteins locally.
11. Production of hides and skins without flaying defects.
12. Creation of employment even for the poorest of the poor.
13. Use of unskilled/semi-skilled manpower with just a week's training.
14. Doing away highly skilled manpower.
15. Low energy requirements based on locally available fuels.
16. Ability to work even if electricity is not available.
17. Ability to process offal from different sources like fishery, poultry, slaughter houses, butcher shops, fallen stock etc.
18. Possibility of scaling up for large throughtputs.
19. Establishing industries on raw materials available from rendering units
20. And many more.

It therefore provides an excellent opportunity for tapping and utilization of vast resources of agricultural residues and animal based offal, which are hitherto wasted.

Chapter 7

Cost Estimates and Profitability

The costs and profitability as worked out here pertain to the prevailing conditions in most parts of rural India (Aug. 2004). The cost worked out is for total package including land, building, vehicle, tools and equipments etc. as shown in Table 7.1.

Table 7.1: Cost Estimates and Profitability

Description	Approximate Cost	
	Indian Rupees	*US Dollars#*
1. Land (1 Acre)	1,50,000	3,000
2. Building	15,00,000	30,000
Boundary wall, Sheds (1500 Sq.Ft.), Office (300 Sq.Ft.), Septic tank (30,000 Litres), Sub-surface irrigation Channel, Overhead tank (5,000 Litres), Compost pits, Water pipe lines, Electrical lines and Office furniture etc.		
3. Tools and Equipments	3,50,000	7,000
Flaying tools, Flaying bed, Hoisting facility on rails, Semi-moist rendering vessel, Meat mincer, Trolley, Shovel, Rake, Tubs, Buckets, Gum boots etc.		
4. Vehicle for collection of carcass	1,00,000	2,000
5. Contingency	1,00,000	2,000
Total	**22,00,000**	**44,000**

Manpower Requirement

a. Manager cum Skilled Worker	1
b. Skilled Workers	2
c. Driver cum Skilled worker	1

1 US $ = Rs. 50

* Such units are expected to be mainly family business.

Working Capital and Depreciation

Manager/Skilled Worker (1) @ I.Rs. 3,500 p.m.	42,000	840 p.a.
Skilled Workers (2) @ I.Rs. 3.000 p.m.	72,000	1,440 p.a.
Driver / Skilled worker (1) @ I.Rs. 3500 p.m	42,000	840 p.a.
Fuel,Water, Misc. and Carcass cost*, if any	1,00,000	2,000 p.a.
Bank Interest @ 4%	88,000	1,760 p.a.
Maintenance and Depreciation (10% on building, equipment & vehicle cost)	2,20,000	4,400 p.a.
	5,64,000	**11,280 p.a.**

Table 7.1–Contd...

Description	Approximate Cost	
	Indian Rupees	*US Dollars#*
Returns by Sale of Produce Per Annum		
1. Hides-900 pieces @ I.Rs.850/piece	7,65,000	15300
2. Skins-500 pieces @ I.Rs.450/piece	2,25,000	4500
3. Meat Meal-15 Tons @ I.Rs.8000/Ton (On dry weight basis)	1,20,000	240
4. Bone-30 Tons @ I.Rs.4000/Ton	1,20,000	240
5. Tallow-3 Tons @ I.Rs.20,000/Ton	60,000	1200
6. Other income through compost, sub-surface irrigation etc.	60,000	1200
	13,40,000	**26,800**
Profitability Per Annum		
Value of Produce	13,40,000	26,800
(Less) Working Capital & Depreciation	5,64,000	11,280
	7,76,000	**15,520**

The total investment on the project including that on land, building and equipment (I. Rs.22,00,000 or U.S $ 44,000) is thereby estimated to be recoverable within a period of 3 years; thereafter the establishment becomes free.

* Carcass is invariably available free of cost in India.

Chapter 8

Guidelines for Construction of Carcass Recovery Centers

There are a few essential requirements, which should work as guidelines while constructing a carcass recovery center. It should be constructed on a piece of elevated land to avoid possible flooding during rains; marshy and rocky lands should also be avoided. The location should be away from villages, towns, and cities. For a center processing about ½ ton raw material (exclusive of hides/skins and rumen contents) per day, about 1 acre of land will be ideal; a 2.5 meter high boundary wall may be constructed around the land with a convenient entry point both for staff as well as vehicles. This prevents the entry of dogs etc. inside the center.

Constructed area will comprise of office room, toilets with bath, septic tank with associated sub-surface irrigation system, dressing room for staff, shed for vehicle, godown for hides, skins and minor products like tail hair, cattle lobe hair, horns and hoofs, shed for bone, bunkers for composting, facility for vermicomposting, sheds for rendering and mincing of tissues, raising animals (if taken up at the center) and for flaying yard.

The flaying yard can be simple, rectangular, well ventilated, fly proof shed with good supply of potable water and facility to wash hides/skins and alimentary track. It has also to be equipped with a hand operated chain pulley (hoist) for a load of 1 ton; the hoist is mounted on a rail of about 3 meters length on which it can move freely from one end to the other (to and fro). Such hoists are commercially available.

Under field conditions, a 7.5 meter × 6 meter shed has been found to be quite comfortable to handle up to 10 carcasses per day. The floor can be of cement and concrete but care has to be taken that it does not have cracks or holes. The floor has a slope directed towards a common drain, which is connected to a septic tank. The four walls (made of brick or stone) could be around 1.5 meters high with the rest made out of fly proof galvanized wire net; the total height of the shed being about 4 meters. A roof of galvanized tin sheet has been found to be very satisfactory. The four walls of the shed should have a smooth plaster of cement and sand mixture. Such a construction is not only cheap but ensures abundant supply of natural light and extremely good ventilation which helps in flushing out any possible bad odors from the shed and also fast drying of its floor after the same has been washed and cleansed. The distance between the floor of the flaying yard and the rail (on which the chain pulley rests) can be 4 meters.

Chapter 9
Tools and Equipments

There are only two equipments *viz.*, semi-moist rendering vessel and meat mincer (as fully explained in Annexure-A, and Annexure-B respectively), which are required in this package of technology. Both the equipments are cheap and affordable and can invariably be fabricated locally; this will do away with import of equipments. Also associated expensive inputs like boiler which is a must to run a conventional dry rendering or a wet rendering system, has been done away with; trained personnel as required to run a boiler as well as conventional rendering equipments, will also not be needed. These features (of the technology) save both on space and investment and make the package a lot cheaper.

Other tools or implements as required are ripping and flaying knives, overhead hoist, gambrel, tail grip, sharpening steel, axe, meat chopper, wooden platform for

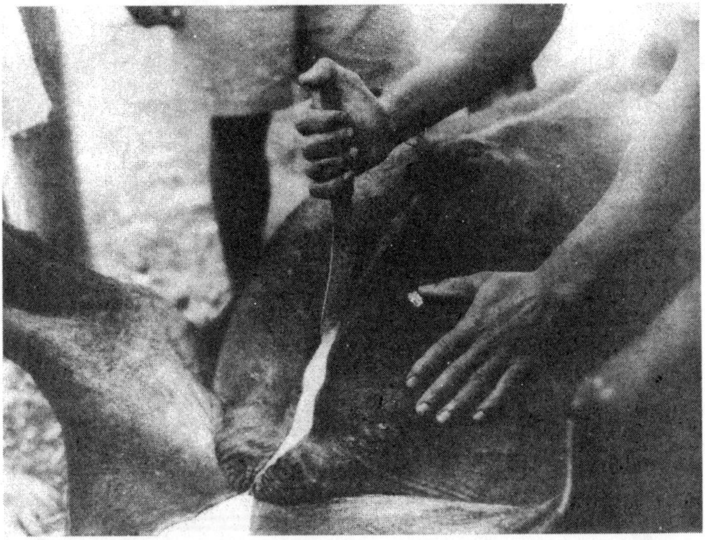

Figure 9.1: Ripping Knife in Use for Ripping Carcass. Ripping knife is a special tool with curved blade and blunt tip.

Figure 9.2: Flaying Knives with Rounder Tips as Compared to the Ripping Knife

chopping of meat/carcass, flaying bed, wheelbarrow, mild steel pan and a dial type weighing scale. General tools like spanners, screwdrivers, cutting pliers, pincers will be desirable to store. Some gardening tools and miscellaneous things like buckets, containers, etc. should always be available at the site.

Pictures of some of the tools are provided (Figures 9.1–9.5).

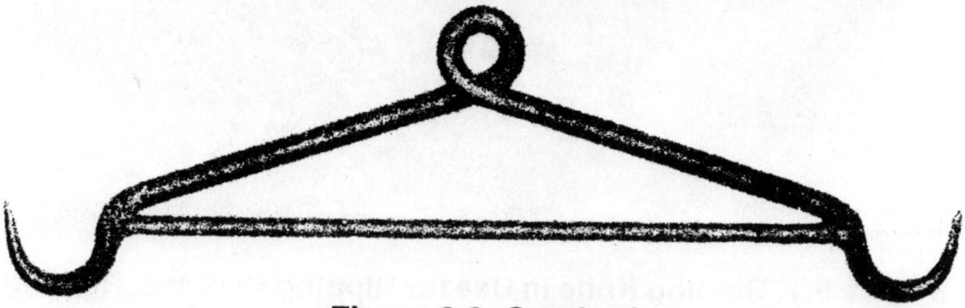

Figure 9.3: Gambrel

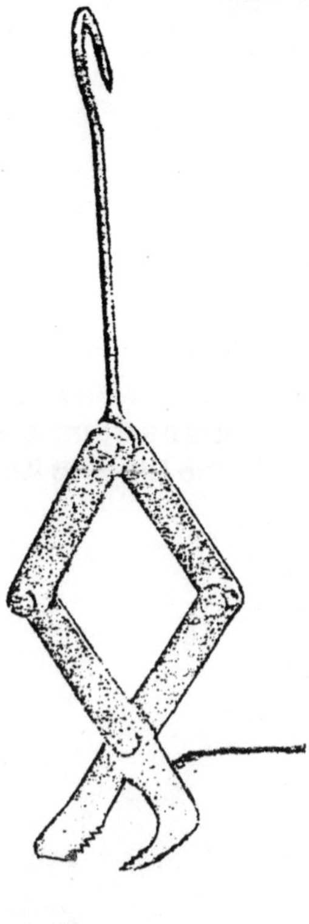

Figure 9.4: Tail Grip

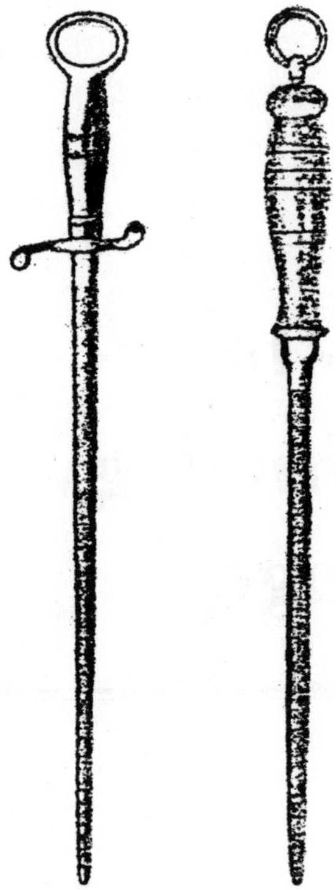

Figure 9.5: Sharpening Steels

The two equipments and the main tools as required for the technology (small throughputs in particular), by themselves speak of low investment needed and simplicity of the technology. The author hopes that these features will make the technology acceptable and popular with the people in time to come.

Chapter 10
New Technology Package

While at the Central Leather Research Institute, the author had drawn up a plan of work to develop economically viable, environmentally clean and eco-friendly technology for the fallen carcass utilization as to be suitable under Indian rural conditions. Most aspects of the planned work were investigated at the laboratory and thereafter, a field center was established at Bakshi ka Talab (BKT) near Lucknow, in the state of Uttar Pradesh in Northern India. The project was funded by the Department of Biotechnology, Government of India.

While this is so, some aspects of the work reported here, more particularly possible methodology for scaling up the technology, interpretation of the data on semi-moist basis and water activity were carried out by the author after his retirement.

The work plan followed at BKT is shown in the form of chart in Figure 10.1.

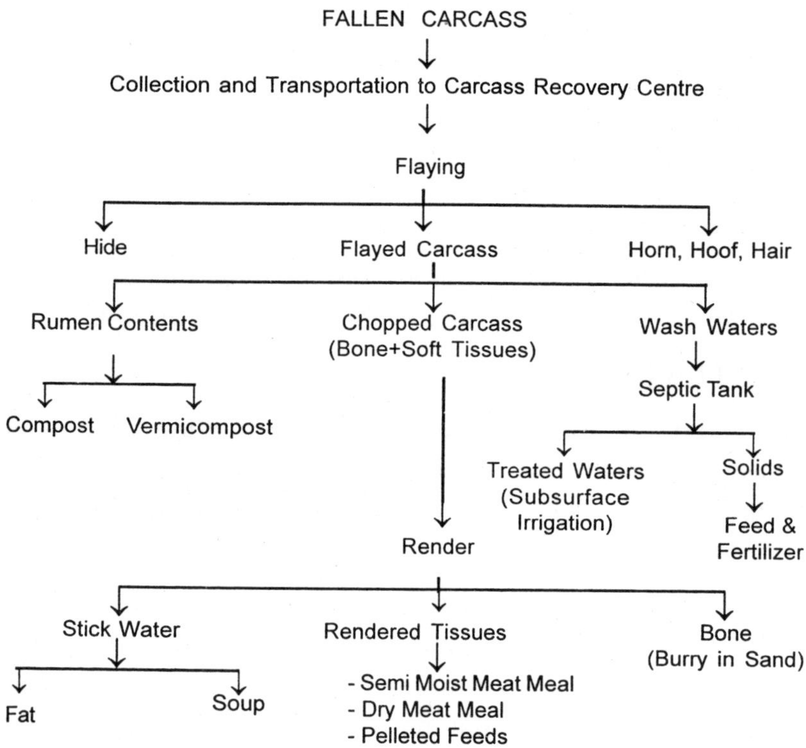

Figure 10.1: Unit Operations for Fallen Carcass Utilization

As is seen from the Figure 10.1, there are six important aspects of successful utilization of fallen stock, which being

1. Collection of the carcass
2. Flaying of the carcass

3. Rendering of the flayed carcass for the production of meat meal/tallow etc.
4. Treatment and disposal of rumen contents
5. Treatment and disposal of effluents of all descriptions
6. Conservation of bone.

The manner in which work is carried out at BKT is discussed.

10.1 Collection

The collection of carcasses may be done in a vehicle as explained under 5.2 or any other affordable means.

10.2 Flaying

After the animal is received at the flaying yard, it is hoisted on four legs (Figure 10.2) and then placed on the skinning bed (Figure 10.3) where it is ripped open and partly flayed.

Subsequently, the carcass is progressively hoisted upwards on its hind legs and flayed as it is raised. Manually operated chain pulley mounted over the over-head rail is used for hoisting and flaying of the carcass (Figure 10.4).

Proper ripping and flaying of the carcass partly on the flaying bed and partly on overhead rail helps in getting well flayed hides without flay cuts and in desirable square pattern. The flayed hide, the tail tuft and the ear lobes (cattle), which had earlier been removed at the time of flaying, are suitably treated and preserved as raw materials. The details of collection of tail tuft as well as ear lobes are available in the literature (Mahendra Kumar 1987).

Figure 10.2: Carcass Hoisted on Four Legs

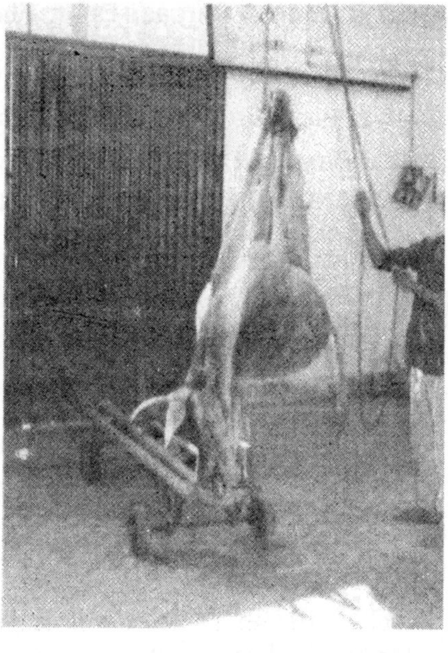

Figure 10.3: Carcass Being Placed on Skinning Bed

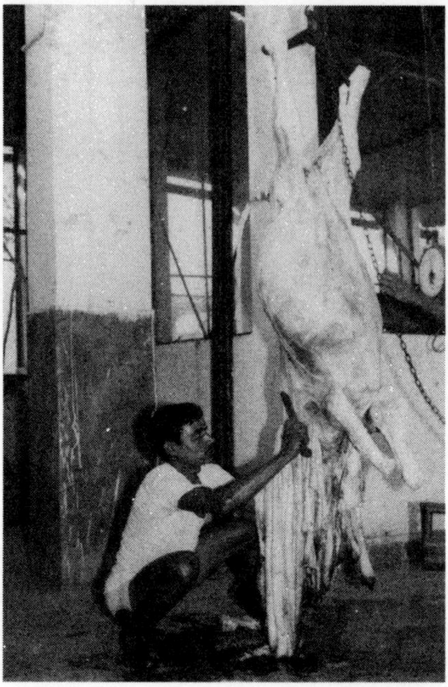

Figure 10.4: Hoisted Carcass Being Flayed

While the flayed carcass is still on rails, the entrails are removed into a wheelbarrow. The flayed carcass is now landed on to a wooden platform laid on the floor, where the same is chopped into smaller pieces with the help of an axe.

10.3 Entrails

The stomach is cut off from other parts of the entrails and the two separated. Thereafter, the stomach is transported to the compost pit, where it is cut open and rumen contents emptied in the pit. This is important because the flies prefer the smell of the rumen contents over meat and so, flies if any, can be kept away from the flaying yard. The empty stomach is washed with water and transported back for rendering.

10.4 Rendering

The chopped carcasses as well as entrails are rendered in the semi-moist rendering vessel, the details of which are available in Annexure A.

The tissues are not only properly cooked and sterilized during rendering but also the meat and adhering sinews get detached from the bones; tallow is also separated or rather say extracted from the tissues during rendering. The horns and hoofs, which have been loosened from the pith and lamina respectively during the course of rendering are collected and dried (Mahendra Kumar 1987) for storage.

The meat meal produced is of high quality; the protein content being around 65 per cent and fat being about 5 to 7 per cent on moisture free basis.

10.5 Mincing

After the raw material has been rendered, soft tissues are separated from the bones and minced with the help of meat mincer. Mincing helps in loosening the structure and reduction of size of the tissues, resulting in considerable increase in its surface area. More details on the role of mincing are available in Annexure-B.

10.6 Dry Meat Meal

Dry meal is produced when mince is dried. Many methods are available for drying such as hot air oven, rotary drier etc. (Mann, I 1962) but drying in an open pan has been found quite satisfactory particularly when the throughputs are small (Figure 10.5).

10.7 Semi Moist Meat Meal

Instead of drying the mince into dry meat meal, the same can be preserved wet as such into "semi-moist meat

Figure 10.5: Drying of the Mince in a Pan into Meat Meal

meal", which finds use in animal feeds in place of dry meat meal. The author has developed methods for the preparation of semi-moist meat meal by preserving the mince with the help of locally available cheap and edible materials like common salt and molasses. More information on the preparation of semi-moist meat meal and its water activity is available in Annexure-C.

10.8 Use of Semi Moist Meat Meal in Pig Feed

In experiments conducted by the author, semi-moist meat meal in combination with other ingredients has been found to be an excellent additive in pig feeds; it had better palatability and gave higher conversion ratio in comparison to commercially available feeds. More details about pig feeding experiments are available in Annexure-D.

10.9 Pelleted Feeds

In yet another approach, rendered minced meat, in combination with other ingredients, is directly used for making pelleted feeds for fish and poultry etc.

The meat mincer itself with appropriate modifications is used for making pelleted feeds. Hence there is no extra investment on this account.

The mince and other ingredients like rice bran, wheat bran etc. are mixed in the form of dough; the soup (instead of water) generated in the process of rendering can be used for making the dough. In this manner, the soluble proteins present in the soup are put to good use. The dough is extruded (Figure 10.6) through the mincer in the form of pellets (Figure 10.7), which are dried or used as such in semi-moist condition itself.

Figure 10.6: Dough Being Extruded in the Form of Pellets

Figure 10.7: Dry Pelleted Feed

10.10 Stick Water

Stick water is composed of 3 components, being (1) fat (2) water and (3) water soluble proteins; all the three released from the raw material during rendering. Water taken between "C" and "D" for initiation of the rendering operation also becomes part of stick water.

The stick water is collected through valves "E" and "F" during and after rendering operation as explained in Annexure-A. The quality of fat in the stick water is of high grade, comparable to any best obtained in any other rendering methods.

In fact, in the semi-moist rendering, the fat is progressively washed out or extracted out of the tissues as opposed to the wet rendering or dry rendering processes where it stays with the tissues throughout the rendering period; as a result fat soluble colouring matter with the tissues dissolves in the fat. Consequently colour of the fat from the semi-moist rendering process tends to be whiter as compared to the other two processes.

The fat is separated from the stick water and refined following simple procedures (Mahendra Kumar 1987 and Mahendra Kumar 1989). After fat has been removed, the remaining part consisting of water and soluble proteins can be rightly called "Soup" and as a matter of fact, used accordingly for feeding the pigs/piglets; it is also used for mixing ingredients for pellets into dough and pig feed ingredients into porridge like consistency. The soup contains about 4 to 6 per cent proteins.

10.11 Bone

The bone has been freed of fat during the process of rendering and separated from meat and sinews as discussed under 10.4, is still wet and needs to be suitably dried; this is done by burying the wet bones in a heap of dry sand. The sand absorbs moisture in few days and thereafter, these can be taken out of the sand and stored for sale. The sand can be used repeatedly for number of times before it is changed with new sand. This is simple, cheap and yet very effective method of drying rendered bones.

10.12 Compost and Horticulture

The rumen contents and so also any organic matter like weeds etc. growing at the center are composted in compost bunkers (Figure 10.8).

The potential of compost has perhaps not been realized. According to estimates, if one cattle carcass is received every day and the rumen contents are composted, one will end up with sufficient compost to manure around 800 rose plants and 4,000 nursery plants (rose). At BKT, the manure

Figure 10.8: Bunkers for Composting at BKT

produced is used at the center itself for maintaining a rose garden and a nursery. This has not only found proper disposal channel for rumen contents, but also added to the beauty of the center and created some extra income. It is estimated that on the basis of rumen contents of just one cattle carcass a day, an average income of Rs.100 (US $2) will be generated everyday from the sale of flowers and nursery plants. As such an approximate income of around US $6 a day could be expected from the rumen contents of 3 to 4 carcasses a day. This will, no doubt, need extra land at the center for raising the garden.

Rose nursery and garden is just one example; depending upon local demand, compost can be alternatively used for raising other flowers or useful plants or sold as such.

Rumen contents can as well be converted into vermi compost; sufficient information is available on this subject. This will yield better income in comparison to simple compost.

Comprehensive information on composting as well as vermicomposting has been discussed in Chapter 12.

10.13 Treatment and Disposal of Effluents

The effluents from the flaying and rendering yards, urine, faeces and wash waters from the pig yard and so also night soil and urine from the toilets are sent to a specially designed septic tank with three compartments. The residence time of the effluents in the tank is a minimum of 20 days. In other words, the tank is so designed that effluents entering into it on a particular day, do not come out before 20 days; so treated outlet water is run into an underground channel filled with stone pebbles, which help the water to run to the end of the channel as designed. Trees like coconut, mango, lemon and many others can be planted along the banks of the channel, which get irrigated through seepage of water from the banks of the channel as seen in Figure 10.9; this system of irrigation is called as sub-surface irrigation. Root crops like carrot, radish and turnip should not be grown on these waters.

Most of the organic matter in the effluents gets stabilized when retained in the septic tank and the bacterial flora is reduced considerably; as a matter of fact, the outlet water looks as clean as drinking water. However, so treated effluents are still rich in nitrogen, minerals and possibly many un-identified factors. As such, irrigation apart, the plants also receive some nutrients. As in the case of rose garden and nursery, this way of disposal of effluents is also expected to generate some income.

In addition, it has been seen (at BKT) that plants irrigated with the treated waters are very healthy, give high yield of crop and are free of pest infestation. Consequently,

Figure 10.9: Sub-surface Irrigation

it has been suspected that there may be certain un-identified factors in the treated waters, which help in keeping the pests away from plants.

Both the maintenance of a rose garden and nursery on the compost and various kinds of trees on treated waters has changed the BKT center into a garden with beauty and fragrance around. It is reported that plants absorb bad odors from atmosphere; it is thereby likely that bad odor, if any, emitted during dressing of the carcass is cleansed up by the plants around. The center is so clean that even house flies are rarely to be seen. This has added respectability to the place.

10.14 Biogas Generation

Biogas (methane) production has not been initiated at BKT. However, the author collected data on the quantities of faeces and urine generated by the pigs and potential of methane generation from this resource as well other effluents. In case, all the meat meal produced was to be used for raising pigs at the center itself, it is amazing to learn that an estimated 75 per cent of fuel needs (for rendering) can be met from this resource. In addition, the slurry produced during the process of biogas generation has been extensively used for irrigation and feed and fertilizer. The profile of the slurry has been studied and found safe for use in irrigation, feed or fertilizer as reported under 13.8.3, 13.8.4 and 13.9 in Chapter 13 (Felix D. Maramba, Sr.).

Detailed information on the production of biogas is given in Chapter 13.

Chapter 11

Wet Rendering and Dry Rendering

In the previous chapter, semi-moist rendering technology has been discussed in detail. The simplicity of the technology is clearly established both in terms of equipment used and methodology of work; one needs only two simple equipments and work details being so simple that even unskilled workers can be trained to perfection in a weeks time.

Complete details of the conventional technologies in all respects like equipments used, work details and kind of training needed for the personnel for satisfactory running of such plants, are available in the literature (Mahendra Kumar 1987 and Mahendra Kumar 1989). However, for immediate reference of the reader, some relevant portions from the literature are reproduced here. This information will provide an opportunity of comparing the simplicity of semi-moist rendering technology as against the complex nature of conventional technologies. Only two conventional systems *viz;* Wet Rendering and Dry Rendering are proposed to be discussed here.

11.1 Wet Rendering

Wet rendering is a process where the offals are cooked along with added water and condensate derived from steam applied under high pressure into the rendering vessel (Mahendra Kumar 1987 and Mahendra Kumar 1989).

11.1.1 Wet Rendering Equipment

A wet rendering equipment called wet rendering cooker is a cylindrical vessel (Figure 11.1) with a cone shaped bottom fitted with a run-off valve at the bottom of the cone.

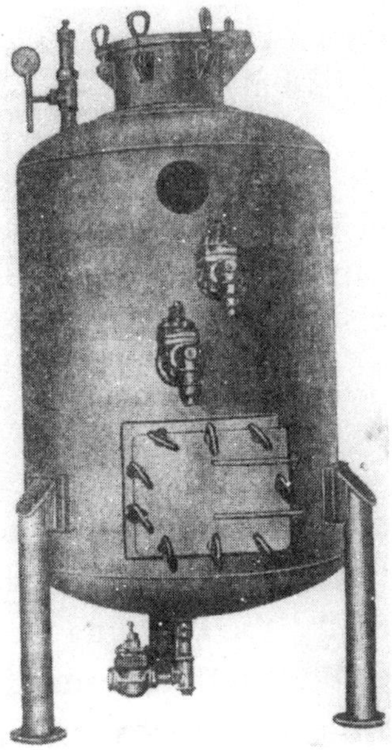

Figure 11.1: A Wet Rendering Vessel

To prevent blocking of the run-off valve, a perforated metal plate is fitted inside the vessel at the junction of the conical bottom and the side wall of the vessel. The vessel is fitted with a charging door at the top for loading of the offals, a discharge gate and two or three draw-off cocks at the side wall. The vessel is also fitted with other accessories like pressure gauge, thermometer, water inlet valve, steam supply valve, steam release valve etc. The equipment is available in capacities of ½ tonne, 1 tonne and so on.

11.1.2 Preparation of Raw Material and Loading

The material is chopped (15-20 cm^3 approx) and loaded through the charging door upto a maximum of three fourth height of the vessel. Smaller the size of the chopped material, better it is for rendering. The discharge gate is tightly clamped and the run-off valve and draw-off cocks are closed. Water, sufficient to cover the raw material, is added through the water inlet valve.

11.1.3 Rendering

The charging door is closed and steam let in through the steam supply valve. The steam out-let valve is closed after about 5 minutes and the steam pressure in the vessel is allowed to raise as desired. Normally, rendering is done at a pressure of 2.8 kg/cm^2 (40 psi). At times, pressure upto 4.2 kg/cm^2 (60 psi) is used to hasten the rendering process. This however, is not desirable for soft and fat tissues. Higher pressure splits the fats into free fatty acids – a condition not desirable. Normally, the contents may be kept at the desired pressure for about 1-$1^1/_2$ hours. However, the total cycle of raising the pressure, cooking at the desired pressure, release of pressure and allowing the contents to settle may take as long as 6-8 hours.

11.1.4 Settling and Removal of Contents

After the cooking is complete, the steam supply is cut-off and steam release valve is cracked thereafter. The pressure of the vessel is allowed to fall gradually till it gets equalized with the atmospheric pressure. One has to be very careful in reducing the pressure which has to be very gradual. Rapid reduction in pressure would cause violent boiling of the contents within, resulting in loss of some product being carried away by the steam and the mixing up of the contents within. The later extends the time of settling of the contents considerably.

The contents settle into three layers of solids (tankage) at the bottom, liquid (stick water) in the middle and fat at the top. Extra water may have to be added at times for raising the level of the fat layer such that the same could be drawn out through the side draw-off cocks. After the contents have settled and separated into the three layers, the fat is drained out through the draw-off cocks and the stick water through the run-off valve. The discharge door is opened and the tankage shoveled out. The tankage contains high percentage of water and needs to be dried.

11.1.5 Centrifugal

In case centrifugal extractor is available, as described later under dry rendering, the tankage may be run in the same. This will help in removal of excess moisture and some fat.

11.1.6 Drying

A number of methods are available for drying of the tankage; the simplest ones being hot air oven drying and tray drying. These are particularly suitable for small throughputs (Mahendra Kumar 1987).

11.1.7 Milling

The dry product is milled into powder. This can be done in a mill as explained later in this chapter itself under dry rendering.

11.1.8 Stick Water

If the quantity of stick water is small, this may have to be disposed off or used as explained under 10.10 in Chapter 10.

In large establishments, however, where necessary facilities are available, the stick water is concentrated in single effect or multiple effect evaporators into thick syrup, called liquid stick. This syrup is rich in proteins. The same is mixed with the tankage and dried. This increases the protein content of the tankage meal.

11.2 Dry Rendering

Unlike other processes, no residual product like stick water is left in the dry rendering process. The yield of the meat meal in the dry rendering process is thereby higher by about 15-20 per cent over wet rendering. Also the retention time for the processing of offals in dry rendering is much shorter compared to wet rendering. Hence capacity-to-capacity, much more quantity of offals could be processed in a dry rendering plant over say a wet rendering one. Moreover, in a dry rendering plant both rendering and drying of the rendered materials are achieved in the rendering cooker itself; this obviates the need for installing a separate unit for drying of the rendered product. For these reasons, wherever possible, a dry rendering unit should be installed in place of say wet rendering. But the capital investment on installing a dry rendering unit is many more times higher than the wet rendering facility and its installation may be justified only when the through-put is large.

In rural areas in the developing countries, availability of such large quantities of raw materials may not be feasible. In the big cities, however, the picture is comparatively different. Hotels are source of bones and other culinary wastes. Fish, meat and poultry wastes are available from meat markets. Number of animals slaughtered is large in the cities. As such blood and some of the rejected and condemned tissues are available in fairly large quantities from the slaughter houses. There may be fallen carcasses available from the nearby livestock farms and animals dying during their transportation brought to cities for slaughter. Some experimental animals may also be available from schools and colleges. If these resources are pooled together, there may be sufficient justification in installing a dry rendering plant. It may however be said that a survey of the resources should be made and their availability ensured before taking a decision for the installation of the unit.

11.2.1 Dry Rendering Unit

A complete dry rendering unit can be divided into two subunits which being,

1. Main rendering unit – the dry rendering cooker.
2. Auxiliary units like prebreaker, hasher, washer, metal detector and screw conveyor.

The auxiliary units are quite expensive and their installation cannot be justified unless the throughputs are very large. As such, their function is described in brief.

11.2.2 Pre-breaker

A pre-breaker is a heavy duty equipment and used for crushing the raw materials, including bones, to uniform small size of around 5 cm^3 (Figure 11.2). This helps in uniform rendering of the raw material in the shortest possible time.

Figure 11.2: A Pre-breaker

11.2.3 Hasher and Washer

The hasher and washer combination (Figure 11.3) is used to hash and wash stomachs and intestines before they go for rendering. Washing helps in removal of colouring matter from the material; this improves the colour of the fat.

11.2.4 Metal Detector

A metal detector is meant to detect and eliminate metal pieces, if any, from the crushed material before the same is fed to the cooker.

11.2.5 Screw Conveyor

The screw conveyor is used to transport and feed the

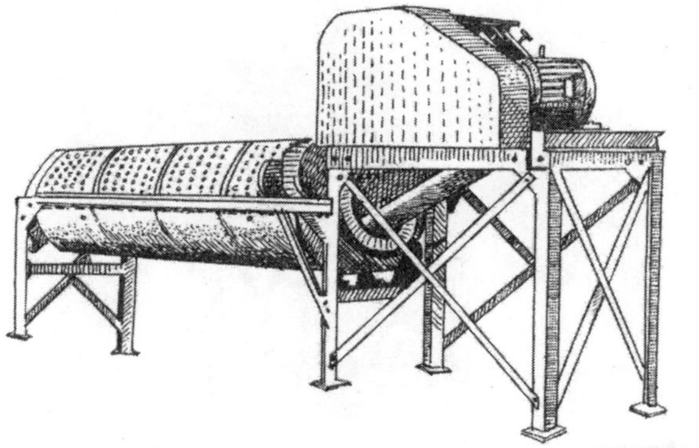

Figure 11.3: A Hasher and Washer Combination

crushed raw material direct to the cooker through the charging door meant for the purpose.

When auxiliary units are not installed, the raw material is prepared manually as discussed under wet rendering.

11.2.6 Dry Rendering Cooker

The dry rendering cooker (Figure 11.4), also called dry renderer, dry rendering vessel or dry rendering melter is a horizontal steam jacketed cylindrical vessel made out of two concentric cylindrical shells of mild steel covered with end plates on both sides, and is fitted with an agitator. The agitator is a shaft passing through the two end plates along the horizontal central axis of the vessel and having either solid or hollow blades securely welded to it. The agitator is supported upon heavy-duty bearings on either side of the end plates of the vessel. The blades are so designed that they continuously scrape the inner surface of the shell while the agitator is in motion. This prevents scorching of the

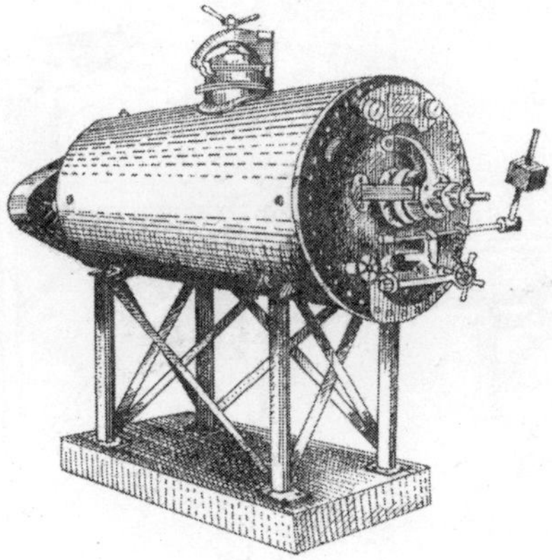

Figure 11.4: A Dry Rendering Cooker

material during the process of rendering. A charging door located at the upper side of the vessel is meant for loading of the material. A sampling valve and a discharge gate are provided at one end plate of the vessel while the other end plate is fitted with the gear drive box and a motor for driving the agitator.

The vessel is fitted with various other accessories like safety valve, steam supply valve, vapour line valve, pressure gauges both for internal shell and steam jacket, steam condensate discharge valve, water jet condenser etc. and is thermally insulated. It is also provided with a starter and a reverse switch so that the agitator could be run in either direction. This helps in unloading of the cooked material from the vessel.

Commercial cookers are available in varying loading capacities such as 0.5 tonne, 1 tonne and so on. Only about 60 to 70 per cent of the available space in the shell is made use of for loading. They are generally manufactured to withstand working pressure of 7 kg/cm (100 psi) with appropriate safety margin.

In a dry rendering cooker, steam is applied to the jacket from where the heat is transmitted to the raw material in the internal shell which evaporates the moisture present in the raw material into steam. The built-in steam pressure and the continuous shaft agitation breakdown the fat cells and disintegrate the material.

To operate the cooker, the agitator is started and steam pressure in the jacket and shaft (if steam heated) is brought to normal level. The cooker is charged with the raw material and sealed. The vapour line valve is opened to let air and vapour escape. The valve is then closed and the cooker brought to a desirable steam pressure at which level it is allowed to remain over a period of time. From then on, steam supply is turned down (but not completely cut-off) and the small vapour line valve cracked to permit the pressure to fall. Sampling of the material through the sampling valve will enable an experienced operator to know whether the cooking is completed, from the slight grittiness and fibrous nature of the cracklings. Slippery cracklings indicate undercooking while disappearance of fibrous nature to touch indicates over cooking. After the charge is cooked, the cooker should be emptied as quickly as possible.

During the cooking operation, the jacket pressure of the cooker is normally not allowed to go beyond 4.2 kg/cm^2 (60 psi) and the shell pressure maintained at about 2.8 kg/cm^2 (40 psi). The time of cooking depends on a number of factors varying approximately between 45 minutes to $1^1/_2$ hours. The higher the pressure used, the shorter will be the time of cooking. The agitator fitted with steam blades reduces the cooking time, ensures uniform distribution of heat through the material and enables the the moisture and heat to pass off more readily (Scaria, K.J. *et al.*, 1981)

A number of volatile gases with obnoxious odours are produced during rendering. These pass through a valve and are scrubbed by a spray of water in a jet condenser. The scrubbings are run out into the drainage. This helps in preventing the pollution of atmosphere with bad odours.

11.3 Separation of Fat from Cracklings

The cooked material called 'cracklings' is emptied into a percolator. The percolator is a bin or receptacle made of mild steel plate having a perforated bottom. It is fitted with steam coils to keep the cracklings hot. The free tallow from the cracklings percolates to the bottom of the percolator from where it passes to the tallow sump by gravity.

Even after the free tallow from the cracklings in the percolator has run out, the cracklings still retain a good percentage of fat and moisture. Further reduction of tallow and moisture from the cracklings is achieved with the use of any of the following methods.

11.3.1 Centrifugal Fat Extraction

A centrifugal fat extractor (Figure 11.5) consists of a perforated basket fitted inside the centrifuge which spins at high speed (between 600 to1000 rpm). A mat is used as a filter in the basket. The basket is loaded with the cracklings and the centrifuge run. The tallow and moisture from the cracklings are thrown out under the centrifugal force into the exterior chamber from where they pass by gravity to the tallow sump. The fat content of the cracklings drops

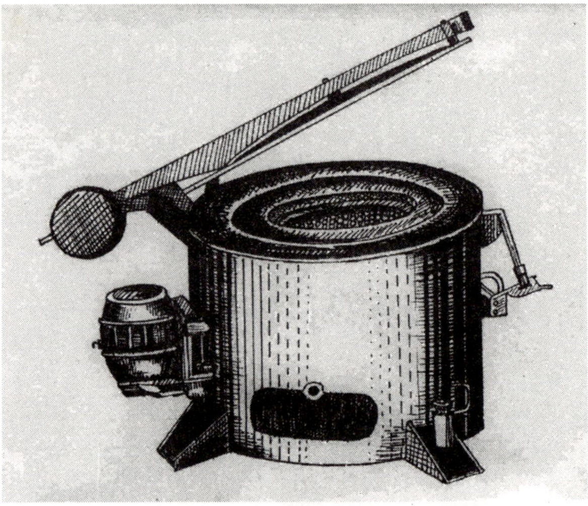

Figure 11.5: A Centrifugal Fat Extractor

down to about 10 per cent after centrifuging. The cracklings at this fat content have a good keeping quality.

11.3.2 Hydraulic Fat Extraction

A hydraulic press is an equipment with a vertical metallic curb and a movable piston inside the curb (Figure 11.6). When the piston is operated, it raises the bottom plate and presses the cracklings against the top plate at pressures reaching upto 280 kg/cm^2 (4,000 psi) thus expelling the fat and moisture in the process. The cracklings which come out as hard cake, are taken out and sent for milling. Under good operating conditions, the cake contains only about 6 to 10 per cent fat.

11.3.3 Fat Expulsion

The fat expeller (Figure 11.7) also called screw press, is normally provided with an arrangement to automatically

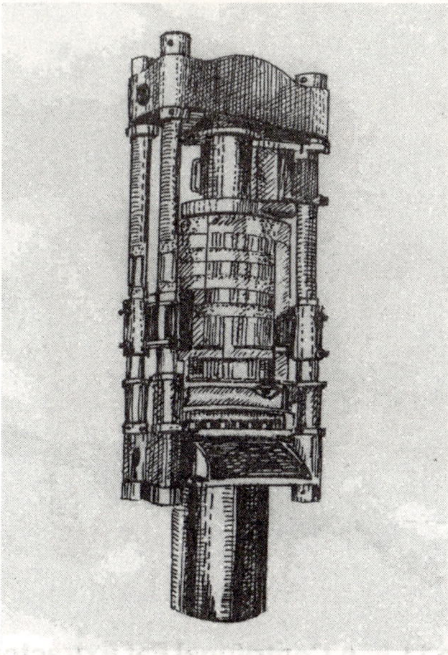

Figure 11.6: A Hydraulic Press

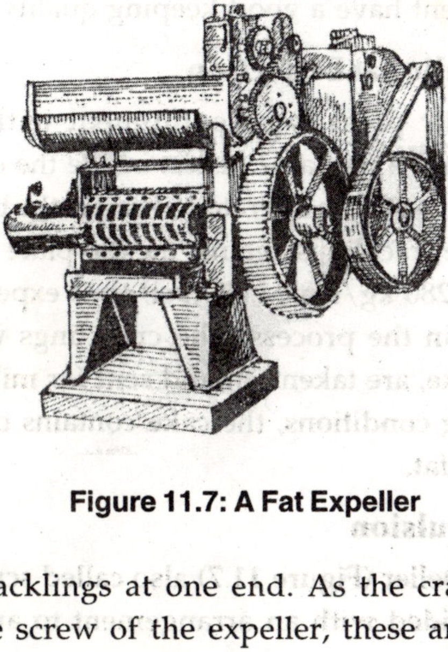

Figure 11.7: A Fat Expeller

feed the cracklings at one end. As the cracklings move through the screw of the expeller, these are subjected to increasing pressure and grinding action whereby the moisture and fat are expelled. The pressed cracklings come out of the other end of the expeller as lumps with approximately 8 per cent fat.

11.3.4 Solvent Extraction

A solvent extractor is an expensive and complex equipment used in chemical industry. Solvent extraction method works on the principle of first dissolving the fat in an organic solvent and subsequently recovering the fat after evaporating the solvent. The solvent is also recovered for reuse. The maintenance and operation of the plant requires highly skilled operators. This process, therefore, is normally not followed very widely. The process reduces the fat content of the cracklings to as low as 0.5 per cent, producing an excellent meal of high keeping quality.

Out of the four fat extraction methods discussed, a centrifugal extractor is the cheapest. Its operation is simple and good quality meals can be produced when the equipment is handled properly.

11.4 Use of Antioxidants

On storage, the fat present in meat meal or carcass meal has a tendency to go rancid. Rancidity is a process of oxidation of fats in the presence of atmospheric oxygen. Rancidity destroys fat-soluble vitamins A, D and E and also affects palatability of the meal. When used in stock feed rations, rancid meal may lead to digestive disorders. Rancidity in meal may be significantly slowed down if antioxidants are added to the raw materials at the processing stage. The antioxidants to be used should be only those permitted under the Food and Drugs Act. They should not be used beyond the permissible limits. Two most commonly used antioxidants for this purpose are butylated hydroxy anisole (BHA) and butylated hydroxy toluene (BHT). Added in quantities of 100gm to every one tonne of fat calculated to be present in the raw material, they prevent rancidity both in the meal as well as the fat produced (Scaria, K. J. *et al.*, 1981).

11.5 Grinding and Sacking

After the extraction of fat, the cracklings are ground to a fine meal. Two main types of grinders *e.g.* hammer mill and cage mill are used for grinding of cracklings.

A sacking unit essentially consists of a 'cyclone' connected to the grinding mill through a pipe. As the cyclone sucks the meal, it simultaneously falls in the sack tied to the mouth of the cyclone and fills it with the meal (Figure 11.8).

Figure 11.8: A Grinding and Sacking Unit

11.6 Refining of Fat

The fat as obtained from percolator, expeller, etc., has high moisture content and also impurities like fine proteinous suspended matter. The presence of impurities affects its keeping quality and hence these are to be removed. Refining may be done in a steam jacketed cylindrical vessel with a conical bottom (Figure 11.9). It is provided with steam supply valve and draw-off valve at the bottom vessel.

Refining is carried out in series of steps as described below:

11.6.1 Boiling

The fat is pumped into the vessel and steam applied to the jacket until the contents begin to boil. Boiling is continued for about 10-15 minutes after which the steam supply is cut off.

Figure 11.9: A Steam Jacketed Vessel for Refining of Fat

11.6.2 Washing

The boiled fat is washed by spraying water onto the top of the fat with a hose pipe.

11.6.3 Settling

The earlier two operations of boiling and washing help in settling of impurities. Proteinous matter coagulates during the boiling operation and tries to settle down at the bottom. Spraying of water on top of the fat further helps in settling of coagulated proteins. Water being heavier than fat, settles down carrying with it any suspended proteinous matter leaving the fat layer at the top. The water and the proteinous matter below the fat layer are removed through the draw-off valve.

11.6.4 Brine Washing

The fat after refining as above still contains some impurities which can be removed by brine washing. The process consists in adding about 10 per cent saturated brine solution (on the volume of fat) to the fat and boiling the contents for about 10 minutes. The salt increases the difference in specific gravity between the fat and suspended matter. When allowed to settle, the clear fat layer floats to the top. The brine and suspended matter below the fat layer are removed through the draw-off valve.

11.6.5 Drying

The fat as refined above will contain appreciable amount of moisture which will cause rancidity if not removed. The fat is, therefore, heated to just below its boiling point for 3-4 hours during which period all moisture evaporates leaving the fat free of moisture.

11.7 Boiler

Equipments apart, a boiler is also a must both for wet rendering as well as dry rendering processes. Steam is needed not only for rendering the tissues but also for drying the rendered stuff into meat meal and also for refining of the fat.

The discussions so far will work as good guide to the reader to enable him to compare the simplicity of the process as well as very low investment required both for equipment, land and so also for the related infrastructure for semi-moist rendering facility as against the conventional wet rendering and dry rendering systems.

Chapter 12
Composting and Vermicomposting

In Chapter 10, use of compost made out of rumen contents has been discussed; possibility of its conversion into vermicompost has also been mentioned.

Compost can be made not only from rumen contents but also from other materials like blood, soft offals of all kinds, hairs etc. if available. Such contingencies may arise at a CRC either because of excess supply of raw material or rejection of some tissues. Vermicompost can be made from dung, rumen contents, leaves, weeds and agricultural residues, if available.

Composting and vermicomposting are of utmost importance to keep the environment clean. This apart, these options are also a source of some income and so also solution to a very critical problem.

Both theoretical as well as practical aspects of making compost and vermicompost will be discussed.

12.1 Composting

Composting is a natural process of degradation of organic wastes of all kinds in the solid-state system, by an aerobic community of microbes which also includes, mesophilic and thermophilic populace.

For best results, certain conditions have to be ensured; the material to be composted should be porous enough for circulation of air and have a moisture content of around 50-60 per cent. For any microbial activity, carbon, carbohydrates (source of energy) and nitrogen (*e.g.* proteins and ammonia) are essential; ideally these have to be in such proportions that carbohydrates are just enough as needed for the conversion of nitrogen present in the waste into microbial nitrogen. Since the animal wastes are of very complex nature, such ideal conditions are rare to be achieved. All the same, reasonably good results are possible to achieve by following a set of practices worked out over the time. These will be described later.

In a properly composted system, temperatures beyond 70°C are achieved. In the first phase, mesophilic organisms are active which heat up the mass upto around 44°C, but the temperature continues to increase and in the process they get increasingly inhibited. In the transition range from about 44°C to 52°C, the thermophilic organisms begin to grow and continue to heat the mass. Thermophilic growth then continues to above 70°C. Most of the pathogenic and thermolabile microorganisms are destroyed or reduced during this period.

The aeration serves more than one purpose – it provides oxygen for continued microbial respiration and removes the end products of microbial metabolism *viz.* carbon dioxide and water. If the latter accumulates, it can make the mass too wet and if this happens, or if the water content of the mass is initially too high, undesirable anaerobic microbial populations becomes dominant.

Microbes apart, fungi and thermophilic actinomycetes also play a role in composting. These are regarded as the major degraders of cellulose.

After the thermophilic cycle, the system starts cooling. New bacterial activity starts after an appropriate temperature is reached. Turning of the compost at this stage not only cools the system but also helps in triggering microbial activity and growth, resulting in the use of readily available nutrients and increase in temperature. As the nutrients are progressively used and microbial activity declines, the compost again cools down. Thereafter, microbial activity again starts and more complex substrates present in the mass, such as cellulose, lignin etc. are utilized; these substrates being complex in nature are acted upon at very slow rate and the heat generated in this activity is lower than the heat loss in the atmosphere. Hence the compost continues to cool down. The active organisms in the cooling phase are usually different from those involved in the heating up phase; the nature of nutrients as available during the heating up and cooling down phases is also found to be different. The final stage in compost making is that of maturing; in this phase macro-organisms such as worms and insects appear in the system and there is considerable predation between the various biotic components of the compost. In practice the composted material is considered mature when it fails to heat up on turning and does not go anoxic (Lynch, J.M. and Poole, N.J. 1979).

12.2 Materials for Composting

Practically all kinds of wastes as available at a CRC such as manure, urine, blood, ruminal and intestinal contents, meat and hide trimmings, floor sweepings, feather, hair and condemned meat could be used for composting. Condemned meat and trimmings etc. should, however be chopped or minced and mixed with earth and evenly spread out at the centre of the compost heap, where the temperatures are the highest. Where quantities are small, chopping may perhaps be a better proposition as mincing of raw meat is rather difficult, requiring power mincers.

Slaughter house wastes apart, some of the other organic roughages, coarse in nature, are essential for successful composting. These could be materials like maize and sorghum stacks, sugarcane trash, straw, wood shavings, broken baskets, waste paper, and the like.

Other materials like vegetable wastes, road sweepings, poultry and fish wastes, over ripe fruits, kitchen wastes and in fact, all kinds of organic materials could be suitably combined and converted into compost.

12.3 Methods of Composting

Composting is carried out by following any of the four methods listed below:

1. Pit Method
2. Stacking Method
3. Vermicomposting Method
4. Mechanically Rotated Drum Method

Methods 1 to 3, are very simple, and no equipments are needed for the same. The first three methods will be discussed in detail. Fourth method is considered out of scope of this write-up.

12.3.1 Pit Method of Composting

Pit method is the simplest method of composting and is, many a times, practiced to convert manure, urine and other materials available at the CRC into compost.

In this method, the materials to be composted are dumped into a shallow pit dug in the ground; complex microbial reactions take place until the material is composted.

Strictly speaking, this method cannot be called as true composting method, as no proper aeration of the mass takes place; it can at best be called as a rubbish dump.

All the same, microbial degradation of the material does take place, both aerobically and anaerobically. The system may still be useful where other methods could not be introduced, even though the end product does not compare favourably with a properly composted one but can still be used as manure. The practice, no doubt, helps in keeping the surroundings of slaughter house clean and tidy.

12.3.2 Stacking Method of Composting

This method consists of stacking or piling of vegetable matter and any offals in alternate layers above the ground. The process is best carried out in masonry bunkers; alternatively the stack could be covered with vegetable matter.

12.3.3 Construction of Bunkers

Stone blocks, cement blocks or bricks may be used for the construction of bunkers, raising the wall above the ground, leaving open spaces in the wall while the same is constructed. The open spaces help in air circulation through the pile.

The size of the bunkers wil depend upon the quantity of the raw material to be composted. Figure 12.1 shows a layout which permits a lorry or a cart to reverse into the bunker for loading of the compost. Perspective view of the bunker is shown in Figure 12.2.

There are four bunkers (A, A1 and C, C1) for holding the raw material. Bunkers B and D are for holding partly composted material from bunkers A and A1 and C and C1 respectively; bunker E further holds composted material from bunkers B and D. The bold lines in the plan indicate

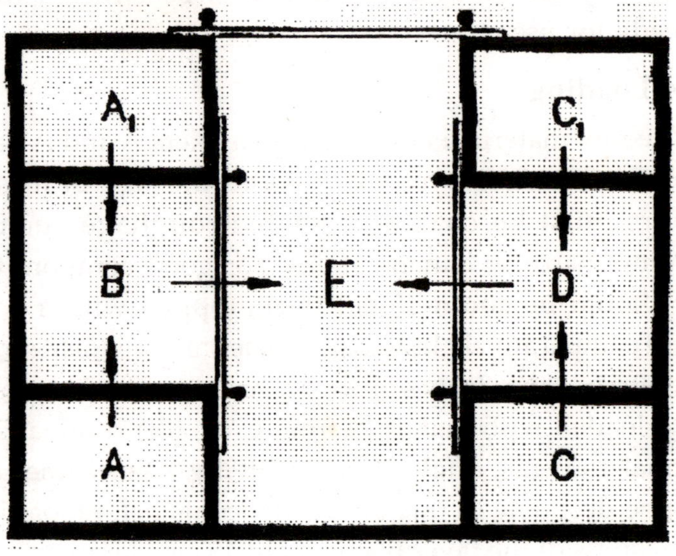

Figure 12.1: Plan of a Compost Bunker

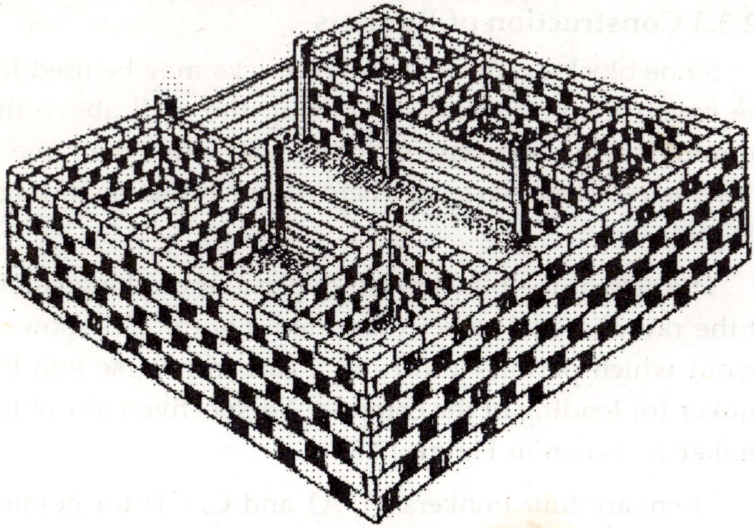

Figure 12.2: Perspective View of the Bunker

masonry walls while white light lines in parallel indicate removable wooden partitions. The floor of all the bunkers is earth only. After the bunkers have been constructed, these are ready for use.

12.3.4 Loading

The raw material is loaded into bunkers A and A1 and C and C1. The first layer which forms the base of these 4 bunkers must be coarse vegetable roughage such as sorghum, maize or banana stalks. For good aeration, this layer should be about 15 cm thick, topped with a 8 cm layer of comparatively less coarse material like wheat straw, paddy straw, grass, leaves or wood shavings. This base layer is now loaded with materials from CRC, like ruminal and intestinal contents, offals or rejects if any, hair, feather etc. It will be desirable to mix all the materials before loading; the thickness of the layer being about 15 cm. Another layer of vegetable waste matter is now topped on the layer of

CRC materials. Such alternate layers of vegetable matter and materials from CRC are repeated until the bunker is full; the last layer being that of vegetable matter. The total height of the stack could be around 150 cm. To prevent drying, the bunker should now be covered suitably with materials like asbestos sheet or corrugated iron sheet – the former being preferable because of its non-rusting nature. When the material becomes too dry, the fermentation is slowed down and it may be necessary to water the stack now and then – in dry climates in particular.

The alternating layers of vegetable waste help in aeration and equalization of moisture as well as its retention all through the system.

12.3.5 First Turning

After a retention period of about 2.5 to 3 weeks, the contents of the bunkers A and A1, are turned and stacked together in bunker B. The contents of C and C1 are turned similarly and stacked in bunker D.

12.3.6 Second Turning

The stacks in bunkers B and D are retained for a further period of about 4 to 4.5 weeks whereafter the contents of the two are turned and stacked together in bunker E; the mix is retained in bunker E for a further period of about 6.5 to 7 weeks. By this time (a total of about 90 days), the contents have decomposed sufficiently and are ready for use (Mann, I 1962).

It may be well appreciated that composting will be dependent upon a number of variables in the system *e.g.* nature, proportion of raw materials, water content, temperature, pH, porosity, air circulation etc. Hence the discussion as offered, could at best, be treated as a guide.

One will learn from experience to suitably combine the available raw materials – both that of CRC and the vegetable matter, as to obtain the best results.

12.4 Stack covered with Vegetable Matter

In this method, the stacking or piling of the available raw materials is done in the same fashion as explained for masonry bunkers; however, the heap is covered from all sides as well as on the top by a thick layer of vegetable matter. Coarse materials like tree branches, long grasses, maize and sorghum stalks and the like have to be used for covering. Clean earth could also be used for covering (Mann, I 1962).

The heap has to be turned at least twice, as was the case in bunkers. While turning, thorough mixing of the contents should be assured to obtain a uniform product. If the process is carried out properly, the other details like the period after which the first and second turning are to be done, the total time taken for composting and so also the temperatures obtained in various phases of the process are almost the same as that in the case of bunkers.

12.5 Benefits of using Compost as Manure

It is a well-established fact, especially for tropical and sub-tropical soils, that composted manures improve the physical condition of the land. The product is a mixture of humus like stable particles useful as soil conditioner. Because of its high organic content, it helps to provide good tilth and water holding and nutrient retaining capacity when mixed with poor soil; as a result, soils otherwise unsuitable, can be put into cultivation by regular use of compost. It also increases the biological activity of the soil and stimulates plant growth (Han, Y.B. 1978).

12.6 Vermiculture/Vermicomposting

Introduction: Vermiculture means artificial rearing or cultivation of worms (Earthworms). Vermicompost is the excreta of earthworms which is rich in humus, nitrogen, potassium and phosphorus. The population of a number of beneficial microbes also increases in the vermicompost; a 4-fold increase in bacterial count and nitrogen fixing bacteria is reported. Actinomycetes, the bacteria that creates humus, increases 8 to 9 times compared to normal compost. The carbon to nitrogen ratio of the vermicompost is also less than the matter to be composted. This may be due to the combustion of carbon during respiration of the earthworms (Edward, C.A. and Lofty, T.R. 1977). Hence vermicompost is a well-balanced fertilizer which provides plants with higher amounts of nitrogen, phosphorus, potassium and humus. The food for earthworms is materials like cattle dung, rumen contents, farm wastes, leaves, twigs, weeds, household garbage, organic municipal wastes, vegetable peelings and other organic materials.

12.6.1 Species of Earthworms Commonly Used in Vermicomposting

The worms which are commonly used for vermicomposting invariably belong to the epigeic category. This is for the fact that in nature epigeic worms live in the top soil and duff layer on the soil surface. These are small, deeply pigmented worms and have poor burrowing capacity.

Epigeic worms are used in vermicomposting because their ideal environment can be duplicated in a bin or bed. They are voracious processors of organic debris, do well in high-density culture and are extremely tolerant to the wide range of environmental conditions and fluctuations.

Eisenia foetida and *Eudrilus eugeniae* belong to the epigeic group of worms. The former is smaller in size as compared to the latter. These are purple red in colour and so are called red worms. *E. eugeniae* has been reported to have surpassed both in feeding as well as reproductive rates compared to other species of earthworms, for the reduction of urban and animal wastes. However, *E. eugeniae* cannot survive even brief periods at temperatures below 7.3°C (45°F). For this reason, *E. foetida* is used in preference over *E. eugeniae* where temperatures are likely to fall below 7.3°C.

Perionyx excavatus is an endemic worm and feeds actively on organic matter high in nitrogen. This apart, *Lampito mauritii* is also used for the purpose.

12.6.2 Construction of Pit/Tank

For the preparation of vermicompost, one needs a storage place like a pit or a single tank or combination of two or four tanks where both earthworms as well as culture media can be stored together over a period of time under conditions suitable for preparation of the compost.

Pit and single tank methods are very easy and simple to be practiced and are the ones proposed to be discussed here.

As a general rule, vermicomposting should be carried out under shed and at an elevated place. Shed can be a thatched roof of suitable size and height. Elevated place is essential to avoid flooding of the facility during rains.

All the working details for a pit or tank for making vermicompost are same except that the pit is dug underground and tank is constructed over the ground.

Most convenient size of the tank from the point of working seems to be 1m(width) x 3m (length) x 0.25 m (height). It can be constructed on unpaved ground using brick and cement mortar as shown in Figure 12.3. This will hold a mix of about 300 kg of rumen contents and other organic wastes. To provide cross ventilation, it is desirable that the tank is provided with holes of 15 mm diameter all around (walls) at 300 mm apart.

Both the tanks as well as thatched roof are constructed in East-West direction lengthwise to protect the site from direct sunlight as well as rain.

12.6.3 Preparation of Vermicompost

Process details are as follows:

1. Spread organic matter like dry leaves, weeds, grasses etc. at the bottom of the tank about 5cm in thickness.

Figure 12.3: Tanks for Vermicomposting

2. Take a mix of about 10-15 days rotten rumen contents and some organic matter like dry leaves, vegetable peelings etc. and spread the same over the bed as prepared under (1).
3. Put $2^1/_2$ kg of earthworms (*E. Foetida*) on the surface of the mix as under (2) and cover with gunny bags.
4. The worms spread all over the surface, start eating the mix and excrete; the excreta is called vermicast. As the mix is eaten, the worms go on burrowing further down and continue the process of eating and casting as they burrow down. Water may have to be sprinkled at the top every now and then to avoid drying and maintain proper moisture content of the mix.
5. Remove the gunny bags after about 10 days; a good top layer of vermicast must have been formed by now. If so, do not sprinkle water for at least 2 days, but cover back the tank with gunny bags. The top layer of vermicast will partially dry during 2 days after which it is removed. The process of removal of vermicast continues until one reaches the bottom. By this time, the worms get accumulated at the bottom layer and infact have multiplied many more times. The process of vermicomposting is complete in about $2^1/_2$ months period.

Vermicasts are small granules which comfortably pass through 2mm sieve; the casts should be partially dried and packed in polythene bags at around 20-25 per cent moisture content. The colour of the vermicompost is something like colour of powder of roasted coffee beans.

12.6.4 Advantages of Using Vermicompost

1. Vermicompost is a natural eco-friendly fertilizer prepared from biodegradable organic wastes and is free from chemical inputs; as such it does not have any adverse effect on soil, plant or environment.
2. It improves soil aeration, texture and tilth, thereby reducing soil compactation.
3. It improves water retention capacity of the soil because of its high humus content.
4. It promotes better root growth and nutrient absorption.
5. It improves nutrient status of soil - both of macro and micro nutrients.

12.6.5 Price

The value of vermicompost for use as manure has already been discussed in detail; because of its innumerable virtues, it sells at around 5 times the price of compost. The retail price of vermicompost being around Rs. 10 per kg and that of compost Rs. 2 per kg in metro cities in India. Wherever possible, thereby, rumen contents can better be converted into vermicompost.

Chapter 13

Biogas from Animal Wastes

13.1 General

Attention is drawn to section 10.14 of Chapter 10, where it has been brought out that almost about 75 per cent energy needs of CRC can be met out from biogas to be produced from various raw materials available at the centre itself. It is therefore, logical that production of biogas is discussed in detail.

In nature "biogas" or "marsh gas" is a product of decomposition of organic matter such as leaves, grasses, wood and twigs buried under marshy places and anaerobic conditions. It is also found as a product of decomposition of the feed material in the stomach of the ruminants. Biogas is mainly composed of methane and carbon dioxide with small percentages of other gases. Methane, in practically pure form, occurs in coal mines and petroleum wells. At ambient temperature and pressure, methane is a colourless and odourless gas and is about half as heavy as air. In admixture with air, both methane and biogas burn with non-luminous flame and so the interest in commercial production of biogas from biomass or the organic matter. In biogas, methane is the only fraction which acts as a fuel; other gases being almost inert.

Methane is the first member of a large family of chemical compounds called saturated hydrocarbons or paraffins. They are made up of two elements–carbon and hydrogen. Methane contains one carbon atom and four hydrogen atoms and is represented by the chemical formula CH_4.

13.2 Animal Wastes: An Ideal Source for Biogas Production

The typical raw materials as available from a CRC are organic in nature consisting of urine and faeces from pigs, rumen contents (RC), intestinal contents, blood, fat, stick water etc. Faeces, rumen contents and intestinal contents are not only rich in carbohydrates but also have fairly good amount of protein. Others like blood, stick water and urine are an excellent source of protein and nitrogen. This apart, the faeces, RC and intestinal contents are also rich in microflora which help in the decomposition of these materials. Moreover, the CRC is a continuous source of supply of these raw materials.

It is well known that proteins, fats and carbohydrates are easily converted into methane under anaerobic conditions. It will, therefore, obtain that CRC wastes are ideally suited for methane production; the chemistry of the biodegradation of the organic matter under anaerobic conditions is well documented and one is advised to refer to the literature for details (Felix D. Maramba, Sr.)

13.3 Yield of Biogas from Different Types of Raw Materials

The yield of biogas depends upon the nature of raw material ie. poultry, piggery, cattle manures etc. (Felix D. Maramba, Sr.). This is well illustrated by the approximate quantity of biogas as available from 1 kg of manure each from poultry, pig and cattle, shown in Table 13.1.

Table 13.1: Yield of Biogas from Poultry, Pig and Cattle Manures

Sl.No.	Source	Biogas Yield
1.	Poultry manure	0.254–0.3 m^3 (8.8–11.0 cft)
2.	Pig manure	0.045–0.064 m^3 (1.55–2.21 cft)
3.	Cattle manure	0.026–0.037 m^3 (0.9–1.28 cft)

This difference in the yield of biogas can be easily explained. The poultry feed contains very little fiber and more of proteins and starches. As such, manure obtained from poultry has more of easily biodegradable components. Cattle feed, on the other hand, has considerable quantity of cellulose – a material which is not easily biodegradable. Pig manure falls in between the poultry and cattle manure in terms of biodegradable components. Information on the yield of biogas from RC does not seem to be available in the literature; however, it is likely that the yield is equal to or slightly less than that from cattle manure (dung).

13.4 Composition of Biogas

The biogas as produced, has a varied composition. There are two main gases of decomposition, which being methane and carbon dioxide with a few other gases in small percentages or even traces. Depending upon the raw material, temperature, pH etc. under which the reaction has been carried out, the percentage of methane in the biogas produced varies between 53 and 70 per cent.

13.5 Optimum Parameters for Anaerobic Fermentation

For best results, the concentration of the solids in the slurry to be fermented is around 10 per cent, temperature between 25°C – 37°C and pH near to 7.5. It is also generally accepted that for optimum results, the ratio of carbon to nitrogen present in the biomass to be fermented should be about 30:1 (Felix D. Maramba, Sr.). The raw material used should be well dispersed in water and the slurry in the digester is agitated periodically. This helps in breaking of the scum which forms at the top of the slurry in the digester.

Commercial systems are now available (Farm Gas Ltd.) where various parameters are maintained within reasonable limits. The temperature in cold climate in particular, is regulated by utilising part of the methane produced, for heating of the slurry which is maintained at around 35°C for best results. The slurry is also agitated by bubbling methane through it from the bottom of the digester.

13.6 Phases of Biogas Production

There are two phases of biogas production – the rapid decomposition of the more vulnerable components, chiefly the carbohydrates, followed by a comparatively slower production of gas from the less fermentable materials. Depending upon several factors, the rapid phase lasts anywhere between 15-25 days, followed by the slower phase extending even beyond 60 days (Felix D. Maramba, Sr.). In actual practice, the raw materials being fermented may not be retained for all the two phases to be completed; rather the process may be terminated at some point during the slower phase of the cycle.

13.7 Biogas Plant

The biogas plant consists mainly of three parts – a digester or a set of these, where organic matter is digested; the gas holder, or a set of these,where the biogas is collected and stored; and the piping system which helps in the transportation of the gas to the place of its use. Depending upon the manner in which the gas is to be used, there may also be auxiliary scrubbers for carbon dioxide and hydrogen sulphide present in the gas produced.

The digester is a tank, normally either rectangular or circular in shape. It may be constructed underground or overground. It should be airtight not only for the escape of the biogas it produces but also to prevent the entry of air into it, since the methane producing bacteria thrive only in the absence of oxygen. The digester should also be waterproof.

There are two types of gas holders – fixed dome type and floating dome type. In fixed dome type, the biogas accumulates in the dome over the digester slurry (Figure 13.1). The slurry serves as a reversible displacement medium. The biogas accumulating in the dome pushes out the portion of the slurry into a higher auxiliary

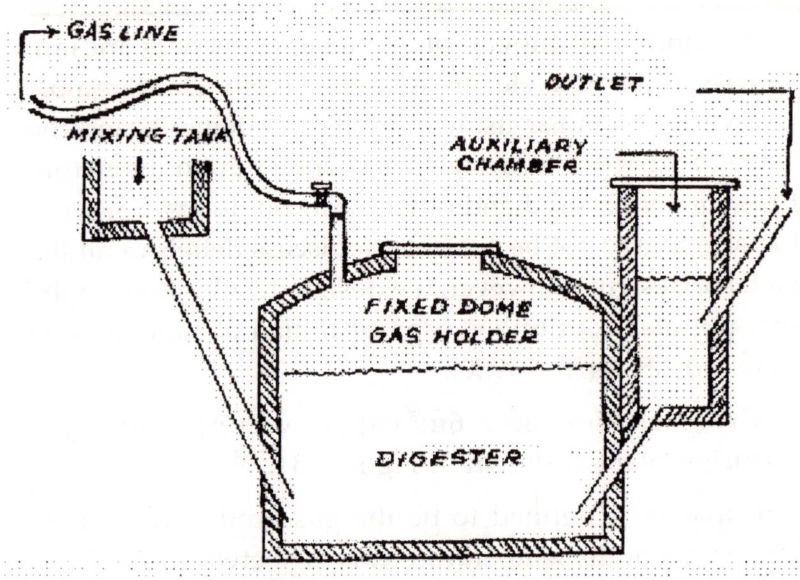

Figure 13.1: Chinese Type of Biogas Plant with a Fixed Dome Gas Holder

compartment. The digester slurry flows back into the dome by gravity as the biogas is consumed.

The floating dome type consists of two parts; an open receptacle filled with liquid and an inverted tank floating on the liquid.

There are two types of biogas plants – continuous type and batch type. In the continuous type, the raw material is fed daily to the plant and production of gas and the fermented slurry is continuous. The newly charged material automatically expels an equal volume of fermented slurry from the plant. In the batch type, there may be several digesters, each producing gas for a certain period after which it is partially or totally emptied and refilled with new gas producing material.

A number of biogas plant designs such as Indian, Chinese, Taiwanese etc. are available (Felix D. Maramba, Sr.). Every design has its own merits and demerits and the choice of a particular design will depend upon the nature of raw materials used and other local conditions. For want of space, it may not be possible to discuss details of all the available designs. However, the design details of one of the most popular continuous type of Indian designs will be discussed (IS: 9478 – 1980).

Cross section of a $6m^3$ capacity continuous gas producing plant is shown in Figure 13.2.

Capacity is defined to be the gas produced in cubic meters/day at the temperature varying between 25 – 35°C. The design is based on cow dung to be used as the raw material. In other words, higher quantity of gas will be produced/day in the same plant if hog manure is used in place of cow dung.

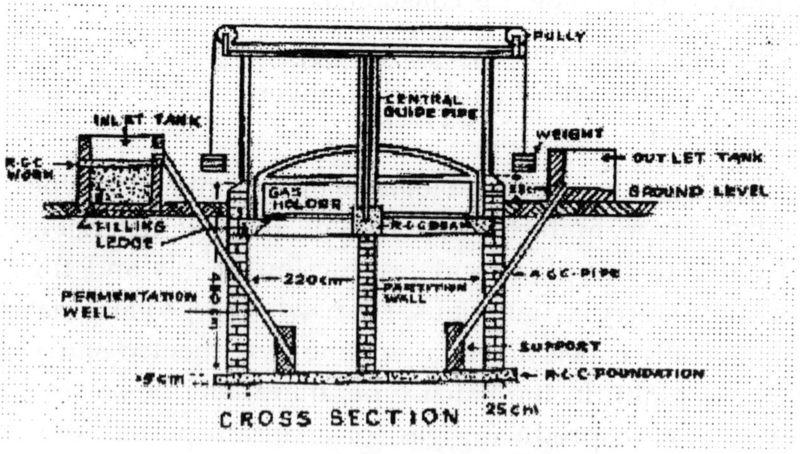

Figure 13.2: Cross Section of a $6m^3$ Indian Continuous Type Plant

13.7.1 The Digester

The digester is a well like construction. The wall of the well is made of brick and mortar, with the thickness of the wall being around 23 cm. Wherever available, stone is a better material against the seepage of water. The well is constructed under the ground and is provided with reinforced concrete and cement (RCC) foundation of a minimum thickness of 15 cm. The well being under the ground, is sealed against variations in atmospheric temperatures. The inner diameter of the well is around 2.3 meters and the total depth being about 4.3 meters. The well is divided into two semi-circular compartments by a partition wall constructed in the middle of the same. The partition wall prevents the mixing of the fresh slurry with the old fermented one. This is desirable for better efficiency of the plant. A ledge at a depth of about 95 cm from the top end of the digester is constructed as an integrated part of the wall of the well.

13.7.2 Gas Holder

The gas holder is a cylindrical drum made out either of galvanised iron sheet or mild steel sheet welded into a drum (with one end open). The outer diameter and flange height of the drum are around 2 meters and 1.1 meters respectively. The drum with its open end as the bottom, is suspended into the well where it dips into the slurry and rests on the ledge. As the gas is formed and fills the empty suspended drum, its upward and downward movements are facilitated by a guide pipe welded at the centre of the base of the drum. In fact, the welded pipe is sleeved on to another rod or pipe which has been embedded into a block of RCC constructed over the partition wall. A stone block can also be used in place of RCC block. The drum has been provided with counterweight arrangement.

The gas produced in the well gets collected inside the drum. The pressure on the gas is equivalent to the weight of the drum and can be further increased by loading extra weights as desired, in the counter weight system. The pressure exerted on the gas helps in its transportation to the place of its use through the system of valves and pipes as shown in Figure 13.2.

13.7.3 Inlet and Outlet Tanks

The inlet and outlet tanks are square shaped with wall lengths of 75 cm and 50 cm respectively. The height of the walls for both the tanks could be 50 cm in each case. The inlet tank is used to feed the slurry in the digester while the outlet tank receives the fermented slurry.

When RC alone is used, the same is converted into a slurry by mixing it with water approximately in the ratio of 1:1 before it is fed into the digester. In the case of other CRC wastes like urine, intestinal contents, blood, stick water etc., the percentage of moisture present is comparatively much higher than the RC. As such, while making slurry out of these materials, the quantity of water to be mixed is to be adjusted. The guiding factor is that the percentage of solids in the slurry is adjusted to around 10 per cent both in the case of dung or other materials (Felix D. Maramba, Sr.and Gobar Gas, Why and How). Care should be taken that no solids are added to the slurry. These settle down at the bottom and reduce the usable space in the digester. The material should be well dispersed in the slurry; finer the size of the material, better the results. The slurry is fed through the inlet tank. A wire gauge strainer should be used to retain any big size material present in the slurry, from entering into the digester. As the digester is fed with the fresh slurry, an equivalent volume of the old fermented slurry is expelled out through the outlet pipe.

13.8 Products of the Biogas Plant

There are two main products available from the biogas plant – the fermented slurry and the biogas.

13.8.1 Biogas

Depending upon the nature of bio-material used, the temperature, the pH and other conditions of fermentation, the composition of the biogas produced may vary as follows:

Methane	-	53–70 per cent
Carbon Dioxide	-	27–43 per cent
Hydrogen	-	1–10 per cent
Nitrogen	-	1–5 per cent
Oxygen	-	0.5–1 per cent
Carbon Monoxide	-	0.1 per cent
Hydrogen Sulphide	-	traces
Others	-	traces

The most efficient use of biogas is in cooking or for direct heating purposes. With properly designed burner, as much as 60 per cent fuel value of the gas could be utilized for heating.

Biogas is non-poisonous with a characteristic odour which disappears on burning. In admixture with air, it burns with a clear, bluish and soot free flame. In its original form, it has a very low inflammability and a burning cigarette will not ignite it. However it is flammable in admixture with air at a level of around 8 – 20 per cent of the biogas in the mixture (Mann, I 1962).

Pure methane burns in a mixture of 91 per cent air and 9 per cent methane. The biogas, however needs approximately 93 per cent air for it to burn completely. For this reason, the normal LPG burners used commonly in the houses are not fit for biogas. Special burners with bigger holes have been designed for use of biogas as a fuel. Bigger holes enable to draw higher percentage of air from the atmosphere, needed for efficient burning of the biogas (IS: 8749 – 1978). With the correct air and biogas mixture, the flame temperature can reach as high as 800°C.

To get an appreciation of the quantity of raw materials required and the volume of gas needed for various end uses, some figures are provided. As already discussed, one kilogram of cattle dung produces around 0.037 m^3 (1.3 cft.) of biogas at atmospheric pressure and roughly 25°C temperature. Corresponding figures for poultry and pig manures have also been given. The availability of RC from an average sized cattle is around 25 kg. Hence RC obtained from at least two cattle heads will produce gas equivalent to around 1.7 m^3 (60 cft.). Under Indian conditions, this volume of gas is considered to meet the cooking and lighting needs of a family of four persons per day (Gobar Gas, Why and How).

For using the biogas for lighting purposes, special mantle lamps have to be used. A 100-candle power lamp, roughly consumes 0.13 m^3 (4.5 cft) of the gas/hour.

As for power, internal combustion engines could be converted for use of biogas as fuel. For doing so, a special attachment is required to be attached to the combustion engine. Before use, the traces of hydrogen sulphide should be removed from the biogas; if not, it will corrode the engine. For this, the biogas is passed through ferric oxide or iron filings which help in scrubbing of the hydrogen sulphide. When ferric oxide is used, the same can be regenerated by heating it in the presence of air and reused. About 0.48 m^3 (17 cft) of fuel gas is required to run an engine of one horse power for one hour.

For gasoline engines, biogas can completely replace gasoline. Gasoline engines could be converted for use of biogas by changing the carburettors.

In case of diesel engines however, diesel cannot be replaced totally with biogas. Some amount of diesel is required for ignition. The diesel engine is converted to a dual fuel (diesel+fuel gas) engine by attaching a biogas carburettor to the air-intake manifold. When biogas is used, the consumption of diesel can be brought down to about 15 – 25 per cent.

13.8.2 The Slurry

During the past, slurry was considered as a product only fit to be used as manure either fresh in liquid form diluted with water or after drying as powder.

However, the excellent work which has been carried out at Maya Farms, in Philippines, has opened a number of other important avenues for its use (Felix D. Maramba, Sr.).

The slurry is an aqueous suspension of solids in a liquid. It resembles dark mud in appearance and contains large quantity of fine fibres.

When fresh, it still produces some biogas. However, as the slurry is exposed to atmosphere, the methane formation stops; the same can take place only under anaerobic conditions. The fresh slurry emits a smell of hydrogen sulphide and is not any more too offensive as is the case with fresh dung.

The slurry is run into a lagoon. As the formation of methane stops, the slurry separates into two portions – the dark solid portion settles at the bottom leaving a turbid liquid sludge layer at the top.

13.8.3 Solid Sludge*

The liquid portion of the slurry or say liquid sludge from the first lagoon is run into another lagoon and the solid sludge which has settled at the bottom of the first lagoon is scooped out and dried in open sun. When analysed, the solid sludge is found to be rich in protein (around 20 per cent), fat (around 5 per cent), fibre (around 10 per cent), phosphorus, potassium, calcium, magnesium, iron, copper, zinc and manganese. The sludge is also free from parasites. Preliminary tests also indicated it to be free of Salmonella. It is also rich in vitamin B12. The analysis shows that the product is not only fit to be used as fertilizer but could better be utilized as a feed material in livestock feeds. Infact, the feeding trial tests on pigs showed very good weight gain when the material was used at 10 per cent level of the total feed. This growth cannot be explained due to the protein alone. It is expected that vitamin B12 and perhaps other unidentified growth factors are responsible for the growth.

13.8.4 Liquid Sludge

About 90 per cent of the total slurry comprises of liquid sludge. As such it poses a big disposal problem when the size of the plant is large.

---

* The data given is in respect of sludge obtained from pig manure.

The liquid portion, when analysed was also found to contain nitrogen, phosphorus, potassium, calcium, magnesium, iron, copper, zinc, manganese etc.

At the Maya Farms, the liquid sludge has been successfully used for the following –

1. As irrigation water and fertilizer – When used for irrigating paddy fields, blue-green algae have been reported to grow in profusion which in turn help in fixing atmospheric nitrogen. The plants irrigated with the liquid sludge were found extremely healthy and it is suspected that other than supplying nitrogen and minerals to the plants, the sludge may also be containing plant hormones and unidentified growth factors.
2. For fish culture – When exposed to sunlight, the sludge is reported to support profuse growth of plankton. Some of the fish, tilapia in particular feed on this plankton. As such, liquid sludge has been found very useful for fish culture.
3. For algae culture – The liquid sludge has also been found suitable for growing Chlorella and other similar algae. However as algae culture also involves further additional operations for its harvesting, drying and bagging, economy of algae culture remains to be established.

13.9 Toxicity of the Slurry

If used for irrigation and fertilizing purposes, the literature on biogas states that the slurry should be allowed to "ripen" before use. When used fresh, the slurry is toxic both to fish and plants. It has been observed at Maya Farms that even very hardy varieties of fish and plants do not survive in the fresh slurry even when highly diluted. It is believed that the toxicity is primarily due to hydrogen sulphide, even if present in traces in the slurry (Felix D. Maramba, Sr.).

When aerated, the hydrogen sulphide gets oxidised to water and elemental sulphur. Whatever may be the reason of toxicity, it has been found that well aerated liquid sludge is no longer toxic to fish and plants. Similarly, solid sludge becomes becomes safe for use when the same is exposed to air and dried.

It is therefore important that the liquid slurry is first aerated well in lagoons before the same is used either for irrigation, production of algae or fish culture; aeration may be hastened if the surface area of the lagoon is increased or by bubbling in air with the help of wind mill etc.

Chapter 14

Possible Application of the Technology in Developed Countries

Although the technology has been developed for small throughputs and primarily for the needs of developing countries, it can possibly find application in some of the developed countries as well, under specific conditions. Two examples are given to illustrate the point.

14.1 United Kingdom

In the United Kingdom, there are number of family butchers spread all over the country; they slaughter the animals in small numbers by themselves and sell the meat essentially to meet the needs of local population. The law demands that the byproducts generated during the slaughter of the animal and dressing of the carcass into meat cuts, have to be disposed off in a fashion that the environment does not get polluted. As a result, the byproducts generated are stored in cold storages, which are later collected by a rendering plant (once a week).

It is not only the cost of storing the byproducts in the cold storage, which the butcher has to bear but he has also to part with the raw material free of cost. This apart, he is required to make some additional payment to the rendering plant; way back in 1990, this additional payment was sterling pound 80 for every one ton of raw material supplied. The blood is normally run out to the local sewage system from such butcher houses; the butcher is also required to pay to the local administration for the extra load of blood he has added to the sewage (Shrimpton, D.H. 1990).

Under such conditions, the new rendering technology as has been discussed, may be found useful. The byproducts generated (including blood) can be rendered and the rendered meat used locally in pig feeds. As a matter of fact, many people maintain small size pig farms in the United Kingdom all over the country; the rendered meat may perhaps be an easy outlet to these farms. The arrangement may prove mutually beneficial both to the pig farmer as well as the butcher; the former is likely to get animal protein at less cost and the butcher may generate some income through the sale of rendered meat as opposed to the free supply of the byproducts as well as additional payment made to the rendering plant.

14.2 Australia

Prior to the introduction of batch dry rendering in Australia in the early 1930's, batch wet rendering was the technology in use. It continued to be used until the 1960's and is still used in some of small plants. In this system, the raw material to be rendered is loaded through a top opening into a vertical pressure vessel known as digester. The digester has a perforated platform sufficiently clear of the bottom to allow space for the collection of water and tallow released from the raw material during rendering, plus the condensed boiler steam introduced as the heating medium (collectively known as "stick water").

On completion of loading, boiler steam is introduced into the bottom (and sometimes from the top) of the digester. The pressure is allowed to build up to that required for the particular processing program, and then held at that for the cooking time. This system produces very good grade tallow, but stick water which collects under the digester platform, contains leached protein from the rendering material in solution. The loss of this protein reduces the rendered solids to fertilizer value, rather than that of meat meal.

At BKT, the process has been modified. Rather than introduce boiler steam, wood or coal burning brazier is used under the digester to provide the heat for cooking process. In this way the stick water consists only of the water released from the raw material which is much less in volume and is saturated protein solution (Macfarlane, D 1993).

In addition to the above, the process conditions in the technology introduced at BKT are such that the rendered solids are fit to be used as meat meal; also stick water being a saturated solution can be used. This aspect has been discussed under Annexure-D.

From the above two examples, one may tend to think that application of the new technology is not limited and is likely to find application world over.

In fact under certain specific conditions, semi-moist rendering technology seems to be the best choice; islands like Falkland Island, British Virgin Island and small countries like Singapore, Bhutan, Nepal, some of the Caribbean countries and many more may fall under this category.

Chapter 15
Possible Fallout of the Technology

15.1 BSE

Bovine Spongiform Encephalopathy (BSE) or also called "Mad Cow Disease" is a disease of cattle which first occurred in the United Kingdom in mid 1980's; to be more specific, the first two cases were confirmed in Nov. 1986 at the Central Veterinary Laboratory in Weybridge.

Any one connected with rendering is well aware of the implications of the problem of BSE to the industry. In essence, because of the occurrence of BSE, meat and bone meal of ruminant origin can no longer be fed back to ruminants, even though the ingredients can be fed to other livestock species, poultry and fish. Eventually this has put limitations on the use of meat and bone meal, resulting in the fall of prices of the produce.

It has been argued that meat meal with low content of calcium and phosphorus can replace fishmeal in aquaculture feed to a great extent. Most of the commercially available aquaculture feeds have very high fishmeal content—some are reported to have as high as 60 per cent. The meat meal produced by the semi-moist rendering technology is almost free of calcium and phosphorus and may thereby offer yet another avenue to the rendering industry for the diversification of its produce in aquaculture feeds. It may be added that meat meal produced following conventional technologies is high in calcium and phosphorus.

15.2 Treatment of Effluents from Other Sources

The treatment and disposal of effluents as discussed under 10.13 has wider implications. Effluents of similar nature containing only organic matter as from meat processing plants, slaughter houses and even human faeces and urine will be amenable to similar treatment.

Treatment of human faeces and urine, for example, can prove to be a boon and be of immense value in improving sanitation in villages, towns and cities wherever sewage systems have not been laid so far. As the package is self sustaining or even could generate some income, recurring expenditure at social cost may not be needed on its maintenance. Hence, once the infrastructure is build up, it may run on its own strength. Broadly speaking thereby, this aspect of the technology in itself may be of particular interest to all the developing countries.

15.3 Raising of Animals for Food Locally

In areas where some agricultural residues like rice bran, wheat bran, molasses etc. and small quantities of soft tissues from the slaughter of ruminants, poultry, pig or dressing of fish etc. are available, a very thriving local cottage industry for raising pig, fish or poultry can be developed based on the use of the available agricultural residues and soft offal as feed. While it helps to solve a very difficult problem of disposal of soft offal, it will also help in the generation of local employment, augmentation of local supply of good quality meat and improve sanitation and environment.

Chapter 16

Scaling Up of Technology

If need be, the proposed technology can appropriately be modified for large-scale production. The author is of the belief that modification costs will be reasonable as perhaps most of the equipments in use presently by the rendering industry, can still be utilized with modest modifications.

Probable flow sheet of modified semi-moist rendering technology for large-scale production as envisaged by the author is offered below in Figure 16.1.

Brief explanation of various unit operations as numbered in the flow sheet is offered.

1. Grinding of the raw material can be done with the help of a pre-breaker as presently followed by the industry.
2. A suitable equipment to coagulate ground tissues on the principle of semi-moist rendering will have to be developed.

Scaling up for Large Scale Production

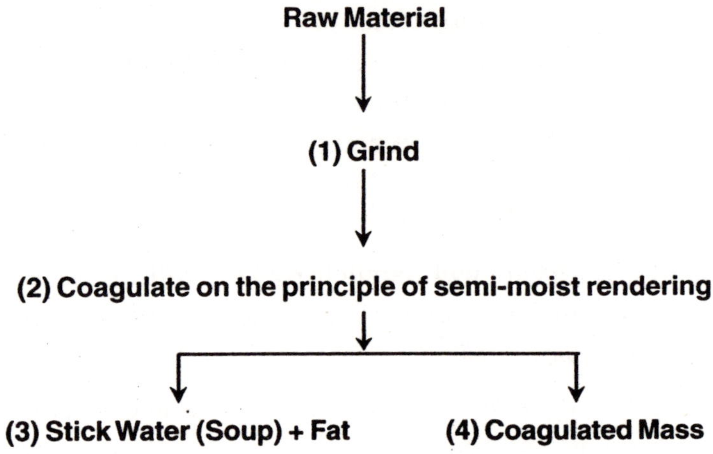

Figure 16.1: Scaling up – Notional Scheme

3. The mix of stick water (soup) + fat is rather a small quantity when compared to wet rendering process. For this reason, it is also a saturated solution of proteins – around 4 to 6 per cent.

   The mix has to be separated into soup and fat. This should be possible with the help of suitable centrifuge like Alfa Laval as is the present practice in the industry. There are various possibilities of making use of the soup as already discussed under Annexure-D.

4. Various products are possible to be made from the coagulated mass; it will have to be decided by the economics and demand of the produce. Some products, which could be made, are enumerated.

The mass can be:

(*a*) Separated into soft tissues and wet-bone; soft tissue to be preserved as semi-moist meal and wet-bone can be dried as dry-bone. However, this option is possible only if an equipment can be developed to separate coagulated mass into soft tissues and wet bone.

(*b*) Preserved wet as such by controlling its water activity; the product will find use in pig, poultry and aqua feeds.

(*c*) Dried using rotary drier and use as conventional meat and bone meal.

From the foregoing discussions it appears that a maximum of only two equipments viz; one to coagulate the ground raw material and another one to separate the coagulated mass into soft tissues and wet bone, will have to be developed for the semi-moist rendering technology to be successful for large scale production. Other equipments are the ones already used presently by the industry.

Anticipated Benefits

A number of benefits can be envisaged by adopting semi-moist rendering technology for large-scale production. A few, which the author can foresee, are discussed:

1) The biggest advantage will be that the produce can be free of Salmonella. This has been discussed under Annexure-C.

2) The second equally important advantage will be on the energy front for the reasons listed.

   (*a*) About 2/3rd water held by the raw tissues gets expelled out during the process of coagulation.

In the conventional processes of rendering, this water has to be dried. Consequently, one will save considerably on energy on this account by following semi-moist rendering.

(*b*) Compared to conventional rendering processes, formation as well as emission of gases and vapours is considerably lower in semi-moist rendering. As a result, there will be big saving on the treatments required for the gases and vapours before they are considered to be fit for disposal in the environment; there will also be associated savings on the equipments, infrastructure and energy needed for such treatments.

3) In the new technology, the fat gets extracted out or leached out from the tissues during the course of rendering; the fat content of meat meal (on dry basis) comes down between 5 to 7 per cent. It may, thereby, be possible that presses or expellers which are required conventionally for expelling out fat from cracklings may not be needed any more in the new package. This again will save on equipment, infrastructure, manpower and energy.

The above suggestions should at best be considered as tentative at this stage and have been offered with the hope that it may help initiate debate and discussion on various pros and cons of the problem. Actual picture about the usefulness of the package can only emerge after such a debate, discussions, experimentation and testing.

Chapter 17
Pig Farming

Cost estimates for a piggery project have not been worked out. However, importance of pig raising can be gauged from the results of the experimental work presented in Annexure-D; on notional basis, the author is of the view that pig raising as discussed in the Annexure is many more times profitable than processing of the fallen stock alone. As such, a carcass recovery center is likely to become economically viable even if, on an average, one carcass is available per day, provided the meat meal obtained from the processing is made use of, for raising pigs at the center itself.

The importance can be realized from the fact that the meat meal available from one carcass will be sufficient for making enough high quality feed as discussed in Annexure-C, for a pig farm of over 100 heads, big and small. With this basic fact, such of those countries where pork is prized, are likely to be dotted with such " Integrated Carcass and Pig Farms" all over. In such a scenario, as on an average only one carcass is to be processed per day, there will be considerable savings on infrastructure investment—land, building, equipment, labor etc. These savings can be ploughed back in creating housing for the pigs and this, in turn, will help in keeping the cost of the "Integrated Farm" within reasonable limits.

Additionally, as the activity will be well dispersed over large area, it is not likely to pose environmental problem, as is the case with centralized pig farming. The income distribution will also be more equitable, thereby ensuring an important social objective.

There are many sectors in the world, India for sure, where pig is considered smelly, dirty and untidy animal. There is also a prevalent notion that the pig "eats like pigs". Such attitudes have perhaps, created a prejudice about the animal and its neglect. In the process, the economics of pig farming has not been understood in such sectors. It will, therefore, be worth mentioning certain facts about the animal.

1. Before a female gives birth to babies, she is called a gilt. After she has babies, called piglets, she is called a sow.
2. Male pigs are called boars.
3. Pigs are tidy animals and would like to be clean all the time. However, they have to be provided a clean place to live and a pond or tub of water to bathe.
4. When the weather gets hot for them, pigs like to cool or else they will get sick. They like to roll in

water to bring down the body temperature, called "wallowing".

5. If fresh water is not available, the animal will like to wallow even in sloppy, wet dirty mud out of desperation.
6. At the minimum, a bore and gilt must be at least six month old to mate. The female gives birth, called farrowing, to a litter of six to fifteen piglets. Average weight of each piglet at birth is about 1.5 kg.
7. The growth of pig is quicker than any other farm animal; when piglets are about six weeks old, they are weaned and the average weight of each piglet being around 16 kg, ten times more than their weight at birth. At the age of six months, each can weigh upto 100 kg.
8. At the prime age, bore and sow can weigh more than 400 kg and 180 kg respectively.
9. Pigs are smartest of all the farm animal. Some of them come and tag their tails when called and others follow their master around, just as the dogs do.
10. The choice of food for pigs can be very wide and versatile. They love corn, cereals, soyabean meal, different kinds of brans, molasses, tubers plants, meat meal, bone meal, table scraps, and many more. This versatility provides an option to formulate feed from the locally available raw materials.
11. In many countries like United States of America, the bulk of the feed for pigs is formulated from corn, cereal grains, soyabean meal and meat meal.

12. For a country like India, many of the locally available materials in bulk like rice bran, deoiled rice bran, various other brans both from cereals and pulses, broken cereals, table scrap from home and hotels, meat meal both from animals dying of natural death and slaughter house byproducts, molasses and more will be ideal for formulating pig feed.

To sum up, opportunities seem to be immense for pig farming for every country. The programme will provide cheap protein, use of local raw materials, environmental cleaning, better health and employment.

ANNEXURES

Annexure-A

Semi-moist Rendering Vessel: Design and Operation

The semi-moist rendering equipment used for rendering of the tissues was designed and reported earlier by the author (Mahendra Kumar and Carioca, J.O.B 2000, Mahendra Kumar, 2001). The equipment has since undergone modification and is reported here. Photograph of the equipment is shown in Figure (Annex A-1).

The function of the equipment can better be understood with the help of its sectional view, which is shown in Figure (Annex A-2).

The equipment is a cylindrical metallic drum with bottom (C) and a circular removable plate (D), which rests on 3 angular supports as seen in the figure (Annex A-2).

Figure Annex A-1: Photograph of Semi Moist Rendering Vessel

The outer surface of the drum has been heavily lagged with a suitable insulating material, to prevent loss of heat. The insulating material has been covered with a thin sheet of aluminum/stainless steel to avoid soakage of the same. The top end of the drum has been provided with a flange with a groove in which rests a circular rubber washer. The perforated plate "D" has been fitted with a perforated vertical pipe "B" as seen in the figure. A water level gauge "A" and draw off valves "E" and "F" have also been provided.

The vessel rests on a movable stand as shown in the figure; the same can be tilted sideways on the stand. This

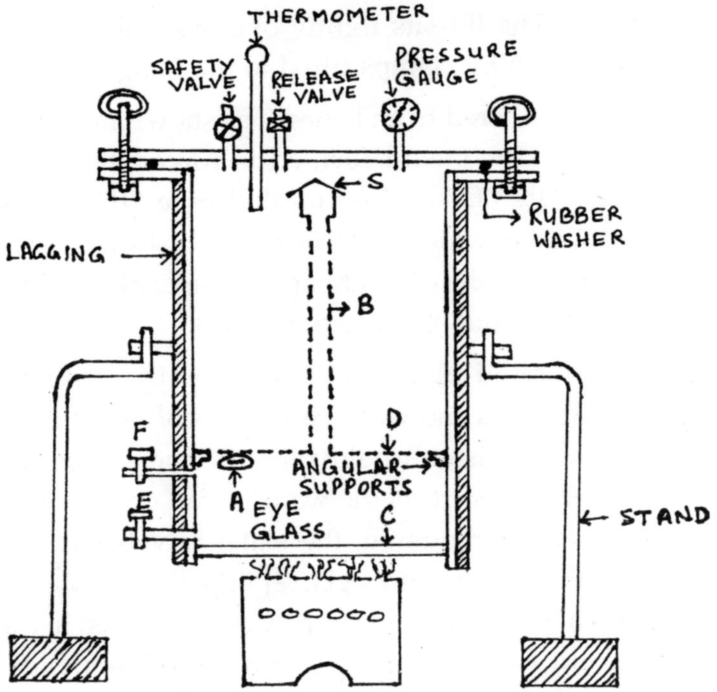

Figure Annex A-2: Semi Moist Rendering Vessel–Sectional View

helps in easy loading and unloading of the tissues into and from the vessel.

Small quantity of water (about 8 cm height) is filled in the space between C and D and the material to be rendered is accommodated in the space above plate "D". Soft tissues, carcass or parts thereof, have to be chopped into pieces not measuring more than 25 cm × 25 cm and loaded into the drum; the same is covered with a heavy lid fitted with a pressure gauge, a safety valve, a manually operated steam release valve and a thermometer. Steam could be released through the manually operated release valve if, for any reason, the pressure increases beyond the one set for the safety valve. The lid sits tightly over the rubber washer, which is secured by clamps fitted to the flange.

The drum is fired from beneath as shown in the Figure (Annex A-2). The steam formed is forced through the perforated plate "D" and perforated pipe "B" and on to the material to be rendered. To begin with, the release valve is kept open to let the air and vapor escape; after all the air has been flushed out, the valve is closed.

The perforated plate "D" and pipe "B" facilitate the circulation of steam and water to all parts of the equipment. The boiling water rises through pipe "B" and strikes against hood "S", which redirects the water to fall on to the top of the material to be rendered; the water travels back to the bottom of the vessel and gets repeatedly circulated, as though it is a boiling water pump as could be seen in Figure (Annex A-3). Consequently, the material achieves the uniformity of temperature all through within a very short time.

As the temperature rises, meat coagulates at around 55°C and loses almost 2/3rd of the water originally held by it; as a result, more water gets collected at the bottom, which in turn, starts soaking the tissues resting on the plate "D". For good results, the soaking of the tissues in water should be minimized. This is achieved by drawing extra water and fat through the draw off valve "F"; water level gauge helps in adjusting the level of the water desired to be maintained in the empty space between "C" and "D". Should the water be allowed to remain in contact with the tissues, there is abnormal softening and higher solubility of the same, which leads to lower quality and yield of the meat meal.

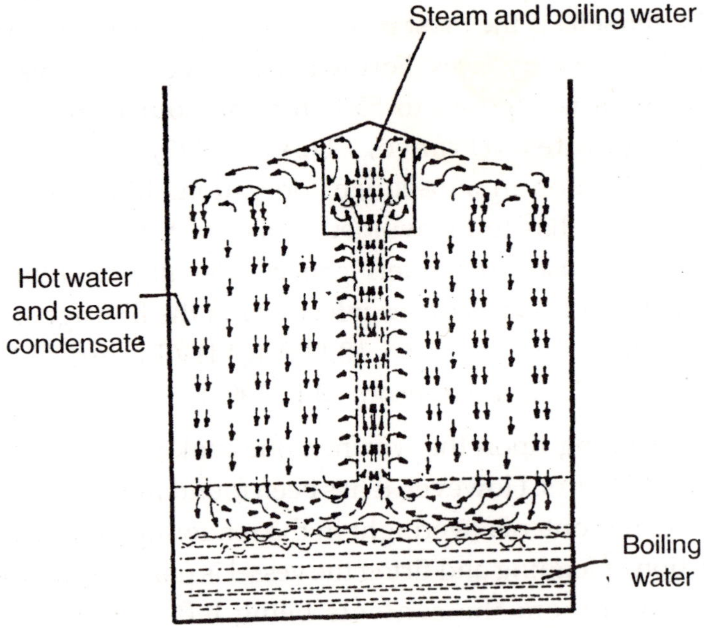

Figure Annex A-3: Semi-moist Rendering Vessel–Water and Steam in Circulation

The rendering is carried out at temperatures varying between 115°C–145°C. After the desired pressure has reached inside the vessel, it is maintained at that upto half an hour and the fire is cut down thereafter, to the minimal; further cooking takes place with the heat locked inside (which has been made possible because of heavy insulation of the vessel as explained earlier) and also from the residual heat being supplied from the brazier. As a result, the fall of the temperature is very slow and gradual, which ensures perfect sterility of the rendered material. If properly fired, the desired temperature of the material inside the vessel is achieved within 45-60 minutes.

Salmonella is the most problematic organism which the rendering industry faces. Fortunately, this gets destroyed if the material is exposed to 55°C for one hour or 60°C for 15–20 minutes (Franco, D.A., 1993). Even so recontamination in subsequent operations like packing, transport etc. has to be avoided. This apart, the time and temperatures used for rendering inactivates all conventional pathogens and even reduces infectivity of the BSE agent by one to three logs (10– to 10,000 fold) (Taylor, D.M., Woodgate, S.L. and Atkinson, M.J., 1995)

Depending upon the weather, one cooking cycle takes about 8-10 hours. However, it has been found more practical to leave the contents overnight in the rendering vessel. The operation of loading and firing the vessel is normally started in the afternoon; the contents being left in the vessel overnight. The vessel is opened the next morning, stick water drawn out through valve E, the contents taken out of the drum by tilting the same sidewise, meat separated from bones (if applicable) and the same minced in a meat mincer. As already stated elsewhere, the water content of the rendered tissues stays at around 55 per cent at this stage; fat associated with the raw tissues also gets extracted and washed out of the tissues through repeated circulation of hot water and steam condensate from top of the tissues to the bottom. The fat gets collected at the bottom of the vessel and drawn out through the draw off valves "E" and "F".

Any locally available fuel like coal, wood, biogas or agricultural residues could be used for firing the rendering vessel. Suitable designs of braziers are available for making use of different kinds of fuels; photograph of one suitable for coal as fuel, is shown in Figure (Annex A-4). In case

Figure Annex A-4: Photograph of a Brazier Suitable for Coal as Fuel

electric power is available, the same can be used in place of the fuels mentioned; in such a case, the heating source will have to be incorporated in the design of the semi-moist rendering vessel.

Annexure-B

Mincing

Rendering makes the tissues soft enough as to be minced with great ease; even the fibrous tissues like tendon and sinews could be minced effortlessly. A simple household 1H.P. meat mincer is able to mince around 50 kg of rendered tissues per hour. The mince (size being 5-6 mm) is dry to touch with open structure and does not get glued into lumps. This is for the fact that water was not allowed to remain in contact with the tissues.

It is important to mention that in places where power supply is either erratic or not available, the mincer can be operated manually with ease by directly attaching a flywheel to the moving worm shaft of the same. This makes the technology independent of power supply, which is very poor or not available in many developing countries. The photograph of a meat mincer in operation can be seen in Figure (Annex B-1).

Figure Annex B-1: Meat Mincer in Operation

Mincing is an important unit operation and plays vital role in the production of either dry or semi-moist meat meal as well as pelleted feed.

For converting the mince into dry meat meal, the same has to be dried. For small quantities, drying in an open pan has been found very satisfactory as has earlier been discussed under 10.6.

Meat is very bad conductor of heat—bigger the pieces longer it takes to dry. Mincing of the rendered stock not only reduces the size but also tremendously increases its surface area, which helps in faster drying into meat meal. While drying, the mince should be raked every now and then; raking is equally important for faster drying of the mince.

Mincing is also desirable for the preparation of either semi-moist meat meal or pelleted feeds as other ingredients of the feed can be easily and thoroughly mixed with the mince.

Annexure-C

Semi-moist Meat Meal and its Water Activity

Scott, in 1950's, defined water activity (represented by the symbol a_w) as the ratio of the water pressure over a food (P) to that over pure water (P_o).

$$\text{So, } a_w = P/P_o$$

Thus, multiplication of the water activity by 100 gives the relative humidity (R.H.) of the atmosphere in equilibrium with the food.

$$\text{R.H. } (\%) = 100 \times a_w$$

When a solute like salt or sugar is added to water, the same (solute) binds with it (water) by increased molecular bonding. The bound part of water does not exert vapor pressure and thereby water activity of the solution is reduced. Bound water is also not available for bacterial activity. Since yeasts, molds or bacteria require a certain amount of available water to support their growth; non-availability (of sufficient water) will hinder their growth. Most bacteria do not grow at water activity below 0.910. Temperature, pH and several other factors can also influence whether an organism will grow in food and rate at which it will grow but water activity may be the most important factor.

Table Annex C-1: Moisture Content and Water Activity

Sample ID	*Description*	*a_w & Temp. in °C*	*Moisture*
A	Mince[1] without additives	0.991/23.8	54.4%
B	Mince (100) + Common Salt (12)	0.854/25.7	50.5%
B_1	Moisture of B partly evaporated	0.806/24.7	44.5%
B_2	Moisture of B_1 further evaporated	0.747/25.4	33.4%
B_3	Some water added to B	0.869/24.8	51.2%
B_4	Further water added to B_3	0.883/26.3	54.5%
C	Mince (100) + Common Salt (10) + Molasses[2] (15)	0.875/25.8	48.0%
C_1	Moisture of C partly evaporated	0.841/25.6	41.9%
C_2	Moisture of C_1 further evaporated	0.719/26.0	27.1%
C_3	Some water added to C	0.883/26.0	49.1%
C_4	Further water added to C_3	0.898/25.6	51.6%

[1] 5mm; [2] 75% solids.

The mince, as explained under Annexure-B, when preserved by controlling its water activity, has been termed as "Semi-moist Meat Meal". The author had earlier developed and reported formulations to control water activity (of the mince), using simple, cheap and locally available raw materials like common salt and molasses

(Mahendra Kumar and Carioca, J.O.B. 2000 and Mahendra Kumar 2001). Two revised formulations, B and C, have since been developed and reported here. To get further insight, the moisture contents of B and C have been varied; moisture and water activity of all the samples measured and tabulated in Table (Annex C-1) and also in the form of graph in Figure (Annex C-1). Moisture content and water activity of the mince (A) as such have also been shown in Table (Annex C-1).

The effect of water activity on bacteria has been studied very thoroughly by various workers. As also discussed earlier, most bacteria do not grow at water activities below 0.910 (Kuntz, Lynn A 1992, Marsili, R 1993 and Grant A. Harris 1996). It is seen from the table and the graph, the water activity of the semi-moist meat meals prepared (B through B_4 and C through C_4) is well below 0.910.

For preparation of the semi-moist meat meal, the solute/ solutes are mixed thoroughly with the mince. The water

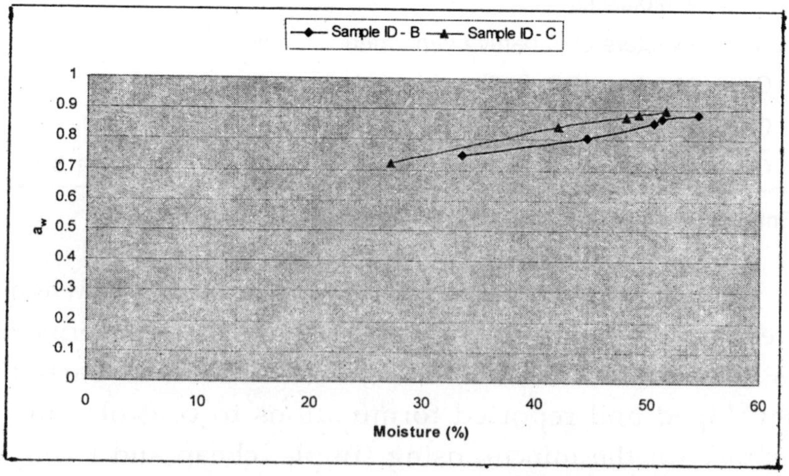

Figure Annex C-1: Moisture v/s Water Activity

activity of B or C being less than 0.910, these will preserve well as such, but it is likely that some contamination takes place during mincing and also mixing of the solute/solutes with the mince. To ensure complete sterility, it may be a good practice that the mix is subjected to a light heat treatment before it is packed airtight in a suitable container. In this form, the mix is sterile and has a long shelf life. The heat treatment is carried out in a pan with good raking of the mix while being heated; raking ensures thorough and uniform distribution of heat and sterility of the meal.

The chemicals used (salt and molasses) for controlling water activity are locally available in most of the developing countries at reasonable prices and are desirable components of the animal feeds. In other words, there is no real cost involved on chemicals, in the preservation of the mince; the salt or molasses could be suitably accounted for, while the feeds are formulated.

Annexure-D

Use of Semi-moist Meat Meal in Pig Feed

Rendered minced meat was prepared by rendering fallen carcasses in the semi-moist rendering vessel as reported under 10.4 and preserved into semi-moist meat meal according to formulation B_1. The feed was prepared daily using semi-moist meal as one of the ingredients; the others being molasses, bone meal and from amongst the locally available agricultural produce and residues like rice bran, wheat bran, corn, sorghum etc. Soup from the stick water was used for mixing ingredients of the feed into porridge like consistency.

The age of the experimental piglets (Yorkshire) was 35 days at the start of the experiment. The feeding experiment was for a period of 12 weeks. The conversion of the feed by the experimental animals to weight gained at the end of the experiment was about 1:1 *i.e.* 1 kg of average weight gain for every 1.0 kg of feed consumed (on dry weight basis); this simple fact looks convincing enough of high profilability of the venture of pig raising.

The average weight of each piglet at the start of the experiment was 6.0 kg; the same being 40 kg at finish; this was more than 10 per cent higher than the control animals. Standard commercially available feed was used for control animals. The results are based on two batches of 10 animals each in each group (experimental and control).

The experiment was mainly conducted to explore the feasibility of feeding semi-moist meat meal in combination with other ingredients; no regard was given for balancing the protein and fiber content etc. of the feed in precise terms. As such, further work is needed to optimize the composition of the feed. The experiment establishes the feasibility of using semi-moist meat meal with very good results and without any problems; the feed was extremely palatable and did not create any indigestion or any other problems even for 35 days old piglets. The animals remained healthy and cheerful throughout the experimental period of 12 weeks and beyond thereafter.

The use of semi-moist meat meal for direct feeding brings down the cost of the feed as one saves on the inputs like labor, energy and infrastructure required for the purpose of drying of the mince into dry meat meal. The semi-moist meat meal can also be used in poultry and aquaculture feed formulations.

The idea of using Semi-moist meat meal looks unconventional but it may be relevant to mention that ensiled fish meal in wet form is in regular use in cattle, poultry, mink and pig farm rations in Denmark for the past about 6 decades now. To be precise, the production of fish silage started in 1948 (Poul Hansen and Nile Alsted).

Feed apart, as mentioned under 10.10, soup part of stick water obtained during the process of rendering can be used for feeding the pigs/piglets (as soup).

Bibliography

1. Campbell, S.G (1995): Private Communication. College of Veterinary Medicine, Cornell University, Ithaca, New York 14353, USA.
2. Edwards, C.A. and Lofty, T.R. (1977): Biology of Earthworms. Chapman and Hall, London.
3. Farm Gas Ltd.: Industrial Estate, Bishop's Castle, Shropshive Sy 95 AQ, UK.
4. Felix D. Maramba, Sr.: Biogas and Waste Recycling—The Philippine Experience, Maya Farms Division, Liberty Flour Mills, Inc., Metro Manila, Philippines.
5. Franco, D.A. (1993): Proceedings of the 54th Minnesota Nutrition Conference, p. 21–35.
6. Grant A. Harris (1996): Food Water Relations. Food Tech Europe, Dec. 1995/ Jan. 1996.

7. Gobar gas, why and how: Director of Gobar Gas Scheme, Khadi and Village Industries Commission, Bramodaya Irla Road, Vile Parle (West), Mumbai (India).
8. Goodman, J. (1991): Private Communication. Meat and Livestock Commission, Milton Keynes, U.K.
9. Han, Y.B. (1978): Microbial utilization of straw – a review. Advances in Applied Microbiology 30, 145/46.
10. IS: 8749-1978: Specification for Gobar gas stove.
11. IS: 9478-1980: Specification for Gobar Gas Plant and Equipment (with amendment No. 1, January 1983).
12. Kunz, Lynn A (1992): Keeping Microorganisms in Control. Food Product Design, Aug. 92, pages 44-51.
13. Lynch, J.M. and Poole, N.J. (1979): Microbial Ecology – a conceptual approach. Blackwell Scientific Publications, Blackwell.
14. Macfarlane, D. (1993): Report on Visit (1 through Nov. 1993) to Central Leather Research Institute, Madras, India. Meat Research Laboratory, Cannon Hill, Qld. 4170, Australia.
15. Mahendra Kumar (1986): Third Course on Animal Byproducts Utilization—Lecture Notes. Central Leather Research Institute, Madras, India.
16. Mahendra Kumar (1987): Processing of Animal Byproducts in Developing Countries—A Manual. Commonwealth Science Council, Marlborough House, Pall Mall, London SW1Y 5HX, UK.
17. Mahendra Kumar (1989): Handbook of Rural Technology for Processing of Animal Byproducts (FAO Agricultural Services Bulletin No.79). Food and Agriculture Organisation of the United Nations, Rome.

18. Mahendra Kumar and Carioca, J.O.B (2000): "Animal Residues Processing for Feed Ingredients" in Recycling Process for Human Food and Animal Feed from Residues and Resources, edited by Carioca J.O.B and Arora, H.L.,Banco do Nordeste and Universidale Federal do Ceara, UFC, Fortaleza- CE, Brazil.
19. Mahendra Kumar (2001): "New Technological Approach to Fallen Carcass and Soft Tissues Utilization For Developing Countries" in Technologies for Value Realization of Carcass Byproducts in Developing Countries—A Handbook. Ramasami, T, Ranganayaki, M.D. and Rajagopal, N.R. Central Leather Research Institute, Madras, India.
20. Mann, I. (1962): Processing and utilization of animal byproducts (FAO Agricultural Development Paper No. 75). Food and Agricultural Organisation of the United Nations, Rome.
21. Mann, I. (1984): Guidelines on Small Slaughter houses and Meat Hygiene for Developing Countries (VPH/ 83.56). World Health Organisation, Geneva.
22. Marsili, R. (1993): Water Activity-Why it is Important and How to Measure it. Food Product Design, Dec. 93.
23. Otto H. Siegmund *et al.* (1982): A Handbook of Diagnosis and Therapy for the Veterinarian. The Merk Veterinary Manual.
24. Poul Hansen and Niels Alsted: Simple, Low-Cost-Production of "Fish Silage Concentrate". Ministry of Fisheries Technical University, Lyngby, Denmark
25. Report of All India Survey on Raw Hides and Skins-Summary and Recommendations (1987): Central Leather Research Institute, Madras, India.

26. Scaria, K.J., Mahendra Kumar and Divakaran, S. (1981): Animal Byproducts – Their processing and utilization. NICLAI Publication – Central Leather Research Institute, Madras.

27. Shrimpton, D.H (1990): Personal Discussions. Nutrition Consultant,"Cragon" Buck's Lane, Little Eversdon, Cambridge CB 7HL, UK.

28. Taylor, D.M., Woodgate, S.L. and Atkinson, M.J. (1995): Inactiviation of Bovine Spongiform Encephalopathy Agent by Rendering Procedures. Veterinary Record, 137; 605–610.

29. Woodley, M. (2005) Discussions via internet. 9, Childerstone Close, Liphook, Hampshire GU 307 XE.

Index